Jacobean Dramatic Perspectives

Jacobean
Dramatic Perspectives

Arthur C. Kirsch

The University Press of Virginia

Charlottesville

THE UNIVERSITY PRESS OF VIRGINIA
Copyright © 1972 by the Rector and Visitors
of the University of Virginia

First published 1972

FRONTISPIECE: Woodcut from title page of
Philaster, London, 1620.

ISBN: 0–8139–0390–4
Library of Congress Catalog Card Number: 70–180964
Printed in the United States of America

To
Beverly

Acknowledgments

A PORTION of the discussion of *Cymbeline* first appeared in my article, "*Cymbeline* and Coterie Dramaturgy," *ELH*, XXXIV (1967), 285–306, copyright by the Johns Hopkins Press; reprinted in *Shakespeare's Later Comedies*, ed. D. J. Palmer (Harmondsworth, Middlesex, Penguin Shakespeare Library, 1971), pp. 264–87.

The writing of this book was generously aided by fellowships and grants from the John Simon Guggenheim Memorial Foundation, the Folger Shakespeare Library, Princeton University, and the University of Virginia. I am thankful for the attention I have received at many libraries, but especially at the Folger, where the staff has been extraordinarily helpful. I can mention here only a few of the students and colleagues to whom I am indebted. William MacPheron stimulated my ideas at the start of the project; Gerald E. Bentley and James G. McManaway made useful suggestions; Lester Beaurline read the entire first draft and suggested many improvements; Stephen Wigler checked references and quotations; and Norman Rabkin wrote a helpful reader's report. I owe most to my wife.

Contents

Acknowledgments   vii

Introduction   3

I   Guarini and Jonson   7

II   Marston   25

III   Beaumont and Fletcher   38

IV   Shakespeare   52

V   Middleton   75

VI   Webster   97

VII   Ford   112

Conclusion   127

Index   133

Jacobean Dramatic Perspectives

Introduction

THERE are many recognized differences between Elizabethan and Jacobean drama, but we still often misread plays from both periods by reducing them to a single paradigm. There is, I think, a need to preserve distinctions, and in particular to appreciate some of the distinctive attributes of Jacobean plays. The first decades of the seventeenth century witnessed a number of developments which were ultimately to change the whole character of English drama, and though their effects upon Jacobean dramaturgy were gradual and complex, they were also profound, impinging upon all the major dramatists of the period, including Shakespeare. It is the purpose of this study to illuminate some of these developments and their effects and to understand the ways in which they can help us interpret individual Jacobean plays.

The most obvious as well as significant development was the rise of Fletcherian tragicomedy. Beaumont and Fletcher were acknowledged in their own time as members of the "triumvirate of wit" which included Jonson and Shakespeare, but though Jonson's reputation may have been higher among the literati and Shakespeare's influence may have been more profound and enduring, it was they who clearly dominated the repertory of the English stage for the better part of the seventeenth century. They were premier dramatists of the King's Men even before Shakespeare retired, and by the second decade of the century their idea of a play as well as their plays themselves had become the staple of the English theater. They had many collaborators; they gave rise to a host of imitators, including Ford, who is not usually associated with them; they exerted a subtle influence on others, probably including Shakespeare; and the characteristics of the tragicomic form they crystallized eventually acquired canonical status for all drama. Both the theatrical criticism and the plays of the later Jacobean and the Caroline periods are thoroughly subsumed by their dramaturgical principles, and by the Restoration Dryden could state quite accurately that two plays of theirs were performed for every one of Shakespeare's or Jonson's combined. It was only in the 1670s, notably with Rymer's attack, that the authority of their dramaturgy began to be questioned, and even then it continued to exercise a considerable influence, especially upon Restoration comedy.

No English dramatists before or since have had so extraordinary an influence.[1]

Another important, if less spectacular, symptom of a change in theatrical taste, particularly in the early years of the century, was the vogue for satiric drama. Initiated by Jonson in 1599 with *Every Man out of His Humour*, comical satires eventually accounted for the bulk of the repertory of the boys' companies and a considerable proportion of the output of the major dramatists of the first decade of the century, including Marston, Middleton, Chapman, and Jonson himself. Harbage estimates that of the fifty-five extant plays which can be assigned with confidence to the coterie theater between 1599 and 1613, "all but a dozen" can be classified as satiric comedies.[2] The effect of this corpus of plays, moreover, was not confined to the years or the theaters in which they were produced: the techniques of dramatic satire unquestionably influenced Beaumont and Fletcher's development of tragicomedy and had a substantial impact upon the tragedies of Webster and Middleton.

Yet another sign of the change in the drama was the rise of the coterie theater itself and the consequent dispersion of the peculiarly heterogeneous audience of the Elizabethan public stage. Though facts are meager and debate is infinite in this matter, there is nevertheless evidence that the audience at the private theater was different from that of the public theater, at any rate had different expectations; that performance by children in the early years had a constitutive effect upon the plays which were produced; and that the resultant kinds of theatrical responses were the ones which were to be increasingly cultivated by seventeenth-century dramatists. Rosencrantz was not the only one to notice the success of the "little eyases," and by 1608 the King's Men had seen the wisdom of acquiring the Blackfriars Theater and performing their repertory there as well at the Globe. For what it reflected, if not for

---

[1] For Beaumont and Fletcher's contemporary reputation, see Lawrence B. Wallis, *Fletcher, Beaumont, & Company* (New York, 1947). Cf. for Jonson's reputation, G. E. Bentley, *Shakespeare and Jonson*, 2 vols. (Chicago, 1945); and for Shakespeare's, David L. Frost, *The School of Shakespeare* (Cambridge, 1968). For two examples, among a multitude, of the absolute dominance of Fletcherian premises in the Caroline period, see the way in which "I. M. S." praises Shakespeare in his commendatory poem in the 1632 folio, sig. [*3], and the kinds of comments upon plays which are recorded in the commonplace book of Abraham Wright, "Excerpta Quaedam per A. W. Adolescentem," ca. 1640 (BM Add MS 22608), reprinted in Arthur C. Kirsch, "A Caroline Commentary on the Drama," *MP*, LXVI (1969), 256–61.

[2] Alfred Harbage, *Shakespeare and the Rival Traditions* (New York, 1952), p. 71. For general discussions of the popularity of satirical comedy, as well as of its nature, see also O. J. Campbell, *Comicall Satyre and Shakespeare's "Troilus and Cressida"* (San Marino, Cal., 1938); and Brian Gibbons, *Jacobean City Comedy* (Cambridge, Mass., 1968).

what it caused, there is good reason for taking this as a critical event in English theatrical history.[3]

The rise of tragicomedy, satiric drama, and the private theater are related phenomena. Certain connections are obvious. Coterie audiences clamored for satiric comedy, and their abundance in the repertory of the children's companies is testimony to their demand. Similarly, Fletcherian tragicomedy, though by no means the exclusive preserve of the private theater, clearly originated there and catered very successfully to its tastes. There are also, as we shall see, less obvious correspondences. Satirical comedy is one of the sources of tragicomedy and has in common with it the creation of a peculiarly self-conscious relationship between the audience and the play, and this relationship, in turn, was certainly encouraged by conditions of performance in the private theater.

Naturally, these developments and relationships are not simple. The rise of the private theater, for example, is a particularly vexed question, because though the opposition between the Elizabethan public, platform stage and the essentially private, proscenium arch stage into which it eventually developed is clear enough, the distinctions and relationship between the public and private theaters in the early Jacobean period are extremely complicated and even confusing. Jonson, Middleton, and Shakespeare himself in the last plays—in other words, the first dramatists of the age—wrote for both, and with equal success. *Every Man out of His Humour*, though it inaugurated a genre which flourished in the coterie theater, was itself a public theater play, and though there is reason to believe that *Cymbeline*, *The Winter's Tale* and *The Tempest* were responding to the stimulus of the private stage, *Pericles*, the acknowledged prototype of the last plays, was unquestionably written for the public stage. Each theater thus pirated from and was influenced by the other, and currents moved in both directions.[4] Moreover, even where hard and fast distinctions are possible, they do not necessarily explain individual works, since an explanation of the nature of the audience and the circumstances of performances does not in itself, obviously, constitute an interpretation of a play.

---

[3] Scholarship on this subject is extensive, but see especially H. N. Hillebrand, *The Child Actors* (Urbana, Ill., 1926); G. E. Bentley, "Shakespeare and the Blackfriars Theatre," *Shakespeare Survey I* (Cambridge, 1948), 38–50; Harbage, op. cit.; William A. Armstrong, "The Audience of the Elizabethan Private Theatres," *RES*, n.s., 10 (1959), 234–49; Irwin Smith, *Shakespeare's Blackfriars Playhouse: Its History and Its Design* (New York, 1964); and Michael Shapiro, "Children's Troupes: Dramatic Illusion and Acting Style," *Comparative Drama*, III (1969), 42–53.

[4] Most critics would, I think, agree that Harbage's discussion of the rival traditions suffers precisely from a failure to take adequate account of these crosscurrents.

Similarly, the genesis and nature of satirical comedy are susceptible to different kinds of interpretation. Both late Elizabethan formal satire and Jacobean satirical comedy can be understood at least in part as responses to contemporary social developments (the decline of the aristocracy, the rise of economic individualism, and so forth), but at the same time their characteristic conventions are highly traditional, even reactionary.[5] Formal satire is indebted to Roman satire and satirical comedies are often deliberate throwbacks to the morality play. The interpretation of these forms, therefore, or of their effect upon other genres, is quite involved.

Tragicomedy itself, finally, has a long and complex Continental history and many roots in earlier English drama, including the whole tradition of what Sidney labelled "mungrell Tragy-comedie."[6] The form Fletcher defined is indeed clear and distinct, and eventually revolutionary, but its immediate effects are problematic. Beaumont and Fletcher's success, though remarkable, was not instantaneous, and their own early plays reveal a network of debts to the Continent as well as to the English public and private theaters. The assessment of the influence of tragicomic dramaturgy upon playwrights in the first two decades of the century, therefore, is difficult, and with a dramatist like Shakespeare, who has a long artistic history of his own, as well as genius, demands particular discrimination and delicacy if it is to be useful at all.[7]

Precisely, therefore, in order to do justice to the dramatists who, like Shakespeare, matter most, the developments of satirical comedy, tragicomedy, and the private theater cannot be treated as reductive formulae. It is the argument of this study that they affected Jacobean drama significantly and that by defining and understanding them we can provide fresh and essential insights into some familiar Jacobean works; but it is also important to remain aware that they influenced different dramatists in different degrees and in different ways, and that the distinctions can be as interesting as the similarities.

[5] Cf., e.g., L. C. Knights, *Drama and Society in the Age of Jonson* (London, 1936), and Alvin Kernan, *The Cankered Muse* (New Haven, 1959).

[6] See F. H. Ristine, *English Tragicomedy* (New York, 1910); Eugene M. Waith, *The Pattern of Tragicomedy in Beaumont and Fletcher* (New Haven, 1952); and Marvin T. Herrick, *Tragicomedy* (Urbana, Ill., 1955).

[7] Stylistic studies such as Marco Mincoff's have been deficient in just this respect. See his "Baroque Literature in England," *Annual of the Historical-Philological Faculty of the University of Sofia*, 43 (1946–47); and "Shakespeare, Fletcher and Baroque Tragedy," *Shakespeare Survey 20* (1967), 1–15.

I

Guarini and Jonson

Guarini's *Pastor Fido*

Т HE idea of tragicomedy as a new and distinct genre was first enun-
ciated in England by John Fletcher in *The Faithful Shepherdess*
and its preface (1608), but the fount of his idea is in *The Pastor Fido*
and its accompanying critical justifications, and it is there that the
implications of the form can best be studied and understood. Guarini
baptized Renaissance tragicomedy if he did not actually create it, and
his influence was enormous. He was repeatedly translated, both in England and on the Continent, and he gave rise to a host of imitators and
disciples.[1] The first English translation of *The Pastor Fido* was published in 1602, and by 1606 Lady Would-Be in Jonson's *Volpone* could
declare that

> All our *English* writers,
> I meane such, as are happy in th' *Italian*,
> Will deigne to steale out of this author, mainely;
> Almost as much, as from MONTAGNIE:
> He has so moderne, and facile a veine,
> Fitting the time, and catching the court-eare.[2]
>
> (III.iv.87–93)

Guarini's "modernism" was deliberate. In the answers he wrote to
the criticism of De Nores and others, he labors to accommodate his play
to classical precepts and concepts, but the core of his position is that
tragicomedy is a new genre, created to serve the tastes of a contemporary
audience. He stresses continuously that both the style and substance of
tragicomedy originated and flourished in response to the demands of
modern audiences and that it is ultimately those demands, legitimately
understood, which justify the form. His critical argument is consistent

[1] For a discussion of Guarini's reputation in the late 16th and early 17th cen-
turies, see Walter F. Staton and William E. Simeone, eds., *A Critical Edition of
Sir Richard Fanshawe's 1647 Translation of Giovanni Battista Guarini's "Il Pastor
Fido"* (Oxford, 1964), pp. ix–xvi; and Herrick, *Tragicomedy*, pp. 130–42.

[2] All references to Jonson's plays are to *Ben Jonson*, eds. Herford and Simpson,
11 vols. (Oxford, 1925–52). Transcriptions of seventeenth-century texts in this
study, whether from early or modern editions, follow modern practice with *i, j, u,
v,* and long *s.*

and carefully worked out. He rejects a moral interpretation of Aristotle's *Poetics*. The end of poetry is not primarily instruction but rather
pleasure through the imitation itself, and as a corollary of this position
he insists that when times change, new genres, of which Aristotle may
not have been aware, must be contrived to respond to them. Tragicomedy is just such a genre, for comedy has decayed into base inter-
mezzi and tragedy has lost its function. "To come to our age," he
explains significantly,

what need have we today to purge terror and pity with tragic sights, since
we have the precepts of our most holy religion, which teaches us with the
word of the gospel? Hence these horrible and savage spectacles are super-
fluous, nor does it seem to me that today we should introduce a tragic action
for any other reason than to get delight from it.[3]

Tragicomedy has arisen to take the place of both the tragic and comic
genres by combining them into a new form which is capable of exploiting, and improving upon, their separate potentialities:

He who composes tragicomedy takes from tragedy its great persons but not
its great action, its verisimilar plot but not its true one, its movement of the
feelings but not its disturbance of them, its pleasure but not its sadness, its
danger but not its death; from comedy it takes laughter that is not excessive,
modest amusement, feigned difficulty, happy reversal, and above all the
comic order, of which we shall speak in its place. These components, thus
managed, can stand together in a single story, especially when they are
handled in a way in accord with their nature and the kind of manners that
pertains to them.[4]

There are two natural consequences of this definition which are
illustrated in both Guarini's theory and in *The Pastor Fido*. The first
is a great and self-conscious concern with plot; the second, to which we
will return later, is an equally self-conscious concern with style. Every
element in Guarini's definition, and especially his emphasis upon the
"comic order," necessarily leads to a plot which is both intricate and
highly ostentatious, and the *Compendium* in fact provides elaborate
analyses of "the proper composition, conduct, knotting, and solution of
a plot, which are the most necessary function of him who wishes to
weave well and artfully a mixture of a dramatic poem."[5] The resulting

[3] Translated by Allan H. Gilbert, *Literary Criticism. Plato to Dryden* (New
York, 1940), p. 523.
[4] Ibid., p. 511.
[5] Translated by Bernard Weinberg, *A History of Literary Criticism in the
Italian Renaissance* (Chicago, 1961), II, 1087.

prescriptions are paradigms for those which were to be devised by tragicomic dramatists from Corneille to Scribe. Guarini's summary of the plot of *The Pastor Fido* in the preface to the 1602 edition is a typical description of a copious tragicomic texture of rising and falling passions, turns and counterturns, knots and unravellings, all leading wittily and inevitably to a happy conclusion:

> In the protasis is contained the marriage arranged by Montano, father of Silvio, and by Titiro, father of Amarilli, in the hope of liberating by this means their country from the horrible sacrifice; the abhorrence of Silvio and Amarilli toward this match; the plot of Corisca to lead into misfortune the enamoured and incautious girl. In the epitasis is contained the taking of Amarilli as a condemned adulteress, the marriage upset, Mirtillo offered in sacrifice, the arrival of Carino, Amarilli unhappy, Titiro tearful, Montano afflicted, and the province grieving.
>
> In the catastrophe is contained the agon between Montano and Carino, the recognition of Mirtillo, the interpretation of the oracle, the death of Mirtillo converted to marriage, all things which had a moment ago been tearful made joyful, the lovers who had up to then been miserable espoused, the province freed from the horrible tribute, and the fable happily changed from very sad to very joyful fortune only through the recognition of The Faithful Shepherd.[6]

The emphasis in this summary and in the play falls naturally upon the recognition scene, for as in many varieties of tragicomedy, the center from which the action really proceeds is the *scène à faire*. In some tragicomedies, however, including those of Beaumont and Fletcher, the recognition is either perfunctory or exceedingly mechanical. In *A King and No King*, for example, it is both: the revelation of Arbaces's parentage is simply a concluding arbitrary turn in a play composed of arbitrary turns. The revelation of Mirtillo's parentage in *The Pastor Fido*, on the other hand, though similarly supported by romantic props, is nevertheless integral to the conception and development of the entire action, and in a note to the scene Guarini justly points to this integrity:

> Here begins the very fine and artistic recognition in this plot, which has all those elements which Aristotle teaches us belong to the more perfect and notable plots. These are three: that it be both necessary and realistic; that it be made not through signs but through reasoning; and that it produce a change either from happy to sad or from sad to happy fortune—which conditions are all clearly present in this recognition.[7]

[6] Translated by Staton and Simeone, *Fanshawe's Pastor Fido*, pp. 177–78.
[7] Ibid., pp. 173–74.

In the same note Guarini goes on to compare the scene to its celebrated
ancestor in *Oedipus Tyrannis* and to emphasize how, as in Sophocles,
the recognition emerges paradoxically and yet inevitably. The comparison is disconcerting but justified, because *The Pastor Fido* does
indeed create a tragicomic analogue not only of the Sophoclean recognition scene itself but also of the kind of organic structure such a scene
entails. In *Oedipus* the recognition is the culmination of a process
dramatized by the whole play—Oedipus's ironic quest for himself.
Throughout the action Oedipus's best instincts lead to self-destruction
and apparent hope begets despair, and no scene demonstrates this
process more clearly or more completely than the scene in which
Oedipus exhumes the final horror of his identity from the messenger
who thinks he is bringing joy. In *The Pastor Fido*, though there is
obviously no characterization comparable to that of Oedipus, there is
a similar process, only inverted. The recognition scene, by revealing
that the Faithful Shepherd is Montano's son and therefore offers Arcadia deliverance from its curse, converts apparent despair to joy and
simultaneously reveals that the whole of the preceding action has been
working towards the same kind of conversion. All the knots of the plot
fall into place in an intricately articulated pattern which transforms
malice and mischance into beneficence and order. Corisca's machina-
tions, the lovers' own misunderstandings (in both plots), the very curse
upon Arcadia itself—all are tragicomically hoist with their own petard
to become the means whereby danger leads to better safety and suffering to increased joy.

This pattern, moreover, goes beyond mere plot contrivance, for it was
Guarini's most significant discovery that the characteristic peripeteia of
tragicomedy could be related to a substantial motif of human experience
—namely the Christian apprehension of *felix culpa*, the achievement
of joy not only through suffering but partly because of it. Guarini suggests the possibility of this relationship in the *Compendium* when he
denies the necessity of tragic katharsis for an audience which lives by
the words of the Holy Gospel, and in the play itself the relationship is
made unmistakably explicit. Thus, for example, when salvation for
Arcadia first becomes evident, Tirenio explains:

> This is that happy day, with so much bloud
> So many tears we did expect.
> This is the blessed end of our distresse.[8]
>   (V.vi; sig. [P4])

---

[8] All quotations from *The Pastor Fido* are from Sir Edward Dymocke's translation (London, 1602).

Shortly afterwards, Amarillis not only forgives but rejoices in Corisca's past villainies:

> I do not onely pardon thee *Corisca*, but
> I count thee deare, th'effect beholding not the cause.
> For fire and sword, although they wounds do bring,
> Yet those once heald to us so whole th'are deare,
> Howsoever now thou prov'st or friend, or foe,
> I am well pleas'd, the Destinies did make
> Thee the good instrement of my content.
> Happie deceits, fortunate trecheries.
>
> (V.ix; sig. [Q4])

Perhaps most explicit of all is the last chorus, which recapitulates both the action of the play and its intended effect:

> O Happie two,
> That plaints have sow'd, and reaped smyles,
> In many grievous foyles
> Have you embellisht your desires,
> Henceforth prepare your amorous fires,
> And bolden up your tender sprights,
> Unto your true sincere delights.
> You cannot have a sounder joy,
> There is no ill can you annoy.
> This is true joy, true pleasure, and true mirth,
> T'which vertue got, in patience giveth birth.
>
> (V.x; sig. Q4v)

These passages are typical of many others in the play,[9] but the paradox which they express is more than a matter of words. It is demonstrated repeatedly in the action itself. It forms the basis of the main plot, as the threats to Amarillis and Mirtillo are continually transformed into a means by which they are protected and drawn closer together. Corisca, a malevolent intriguer who is the unwitting agent of Providence, is the objectification of this movement. All of her plots not only misfire, but recoil, as her desire to separate the lovers is consistently the instrument that unites them and helps bring them to the marriage which is at once a fulfillment and a redemption. In the subplot, the paradox of love is even more acute, functioning like a dramatized con-

---

[9] References to the paradoxes of Providence in the play are profuse. See, e.g., I, iv, sigs. Dv–D2; II, i, sig. E3; III, v, sig. Iv; III, vi, sigs. 12–12v; III, vii, sig. [14]; IV, v, sig. L4v; IV, ix, sig. Nv; V, v, sigs. P2–P2v; V, vi, sig. P3v. In addition, see the choruses at the end of each act of the play.

ceit. Dorinda is in love with Silvio, but he is a votary of the hunt and
spurns her with deliberate arrogance and cruelty. One day, however,
fresh from a victorious foray against the Erimanthian boar, he accidentally wounds Dorinda in the woods, and of course immediately falls in
love with her. Her suffering by his hand transforms him, and the arrow
he has loosed upon her leaves its shaft in his own heart. He is the happy
prey of his own hunt,[10] and subsequently he himself finds and admin-
isters the remedy—an old hunting potion—which cures Dorinda of her
wound and confirms his conversion to love.

Ultimately, the peculiar power of paradox in *The Pastor Fido* is
probably derived from Guarini's very conception of tragicomedy as an
aesthetic kind. As Guarini intended, the inevitable effect of an action
which constantly juxtaposes extremes and which arouses our passions
only to allay them is to draw attention to the dramatist himself and to
make us consciously aware of the play as a play. This consciousness
creates a distance between us and the action and thereby insulates our
feelings, allowing us to observe the comic resolutions as well as to
rejoice in them. Repeatedly in the play we are meant to admire and
wonder at not only the marvelous oppositions of events and feelings
which are depicted but also the art which depicts them. Indeed, wonder
is often at once the subject and the effect of a scene—and preminently
of the recognition scene. Eventually this kind of conflation can lead—as
it does in Shakespeare—to an identification of the dramatist with Providence and of his plot with the workings of that Providence. Guarini
does not make this identification, but both his theory and his play suggest its dramatic potentialities. His criticism is emphatic about the
primarily aesthetic function of the tragicomic genre (and indeed, of all
art) and *The Pastor Fido* itself clearly and deliberately tries to make
that function a natural expression of the providential ideas it treats.

A second necessary feature of Guarini's conception of the tragicomic
genre is a self-conscious emphasis upon style, and like the corollary
emphasis upon plot, it too has an organic function in the play. In the
Compendium Guarini explains that the "normal and chief style of
tragicomedy" is

the magnificent, which, when accompanied with the grave, becomes the
norm of tragedy, but when mingled with the polished, makes the combination fitting to tragicomic poetry. Since it deals with great persons and heroes,
humble diction is unfitting, and since it is not concerned with the terrible

---

[10] The episode is saturated with paradoxical word play, e.g.:

Sil. Tell me, Dorinda, doth thy wound still pricke?
Dor. It doth; but in thine armes my lovelie treasure
    I hold ev'n pricking dear, and death a pleasure.

and the horrible, but rather avoids it, it abandons the grave and employs the sweet, which modifies the greatness and sublimity that is proper to pure tragedy.[11]

In another passage Guarini describes tragicomic style in similar terms:

just as it is not distant from ordinary speech, so it is not close to that of the people; not so elaborate that the stage would be averse to it nor so vulgar that the theater would despise it, but it can at the same time be performed without tediousness and read without effort. And this is that nobility of language which, if I be not mistaken, Aristotle taught us—which, being outside common usage, insofar as it departs from proper meaning acquires rarity, and insofar as it approaches common usage becomes proper.[12]

The primary purpose of this kind of style is to display itself, to draw attention to its own polish. The approach to common usage of which Guarini speaks is present, but its ultimate effect, curiously, is to make the style even more self-conscious and "rare." Outside of the drama the nearest analogue to such a style is opera, and it may partly have been its analogies to opera (both theoretical and practical) which made *The Pastor Fido* so influential in the seventeenth and eighteenth centuries, particularly on the Continent, where opera flourished. In any event *The Pastor Fido* is filled with long speeches which are declamatory and which call attention to their own virtuosity. In Act I, scene iii Corisca has a long, ratiocinative speech which plays ironically upon the *topoi* of honor and constancy in women. Later in the same act (scene v) the Satyr declaims a satirical set piece upon women's cosmetics. In Act II (scenes i and v) both Mirtillo and Amarillis indulge in lengthy pastoral descriptions, Amarillis on the theme of humble contentment. In Act III they take part in a highly stylized game of blindman's buff (scene ii) and then engage in a lengthy debate (scene iii) which is marked as much by displays of wit as of passion. Shortly afterwards (scene v) Corisca tries to sway Amarillis with a declamation upon *carpe diem*, and later (scene viii), after being duped into thinking that Amarillis is lustful, Mirtillo exercises himself at length with fantasies of despair and revenge. In Act IV, scene viii, in an extremely stylized episode, words from a soliloquy by Silvio are repeated by "Eccho *within*," the words which are echoed anticipating his imminent fall to love. Finally, the multiplicity of reversals and recognitions in Act V highlight and counterpoint various passionate soliloquies by the fathers of the lovers and by the priests and prophet: Montano, for example, declaims de-

---

[11] Gilbert, op. cit., p. 525.
[12] Weinberg, op. cit., p. 1088.

spairingly about the inscrutability and cruelty of Providence (scene v),
and Tirenio follows by proclaiming its joyousness and benevolence
(scene vi).

All of these speeches are elaborate and clearly conscious of their own
artifice. If they are not exactly arias, they are in the same style, and in a
detailed note to the blindman's buff scene, it is evident that Guarini
thought of the production of the play in explicitly operatic and choreographic terms:

> It is necessary to warn the reader that all the movements that are customary
> in such a disordered and casual game are, in this scene, studied with metre
> and harmony, in such a way that it is not less a dance than a game, which
> imitates the ancient custom of the Greeks and Romans, as Lucian clearly
> shows in his excellent treatise on the art of dancing. . . . Nor can I pass over
> in silence the way in which our poet composed the words of this dance, which
> was thus: First, he had the dance composed by an expert in such exercises,
> he devising a way of imitating the motions and gestures that are customarily
> used in an ordinary game of blindman's buff. The dance done, it was put
> to music by Luzzasco, the most excellent musician of our time. Then the
> poet wrote the words under the notes of music, which caused the diversity
> of the verses, now of five syllables, now of seven, now of eight, now of
> eleven, according to what satisfied the requirements of the notes. It was
> a thing that appeared impossible; and if he had not done it many times with
> so much greater difficulty when in other dances he was not master of the
> invention as he was in this one, he would not have believed it possible. For
> in those dances he had not only the trouble of putting the words under the
> notes, but of inventing the dance movements which they would fit and
> managing the plot as well.[13]

The stylization which this description calls for has obvious analogies
with sixteenth-century Italian opera as well as with the work of English
coterie dramatists like Lyly, but its association specifically with the genre
of tragicomedy is an harbinger of many developments in seventeenth-
century drama. In plays like Beaumont and Fletcher's a similar self-
conscious display of language and spectacle becomes in itself the basic
motive of the action, while in Shakespeare's last plays and some of his
earlier comedies such displays are usually part of integral thematic
concerns. Guarini does not relate his rhetorical and theatrical ostenta-
tion to his themes as directly or comprehensively as Shakespeare does—
there is barely a suggestion, for example, of Shakespeare's continuing
preoccupation with the antithesis of nature and art—but neither does
he exploit it largely for its own sake as Beaumont and Fletcher often
do. As with his plotting, though less explicitly, he creates responses of

13 Staton and Simeone, op. cit., pp. 169–70.

wonder and admiration through our very admiration for his tragi-comic polish, and these responses become part of the effect of the marvelous action which is the play's subject. And it was the marvelous, the *Compendium* makes clear, which Guarini saw as the true object of tragicomedy.

Beyond all of Guarini's Aristotelian maneuverings in the *Compendium* is really an essentially Horatian and Renaissance concept of decorum. For an age supported by an understanding of the Scriptures and aware of its own artistic history, Guarini considered no genre more appropriate and inevitable than that of tragicomedy. Self-consciously wonderful, it expressed at once the marvelous Providence of nature and art. *The Pastor Fido* itself is not a great exemplification of the form, but it is its paradigm, and together with Guarini's theory, it made a new dramatic form available to succeeding dramatists both on the Continent and in England.

Jonson's *Every Man out of His Humour* and *Cynthia's Revels*

Guarini's counterpart in England was Ben Jonson. Jonson had none of Guarini's romantic dispositions, and the genre he established, satirical comedy, is in many respects the polar opposite of tragicomedy. Where tragicomedy is designed to celebrate man's deliverance from evil and sorrow and presents an action in which oppositions are being continuously transformed, satirical comedy is constructed to expose man's evil condition and its vision of the oppositions which govern man's behavior is characteristically static. Nevertheless, in equally important respects, both authors were similarly revolutionary. *Every Man Out* was Jonson's first published play, probably his first substantial theatrical success, and he was as conscious as Guarini that he was doing something new.[14] The motto from Horace on the title page of the first edition (1600) announces: *Non aliena meo pressi pede* / *si proprius stes,* / *Te capient magis* / *& decies repetita placebunt* [I did not follow in others' footsteps. If you examine this closely, it will please more; and, though called for ten times again, will always please]. Undoubtedly part of what Jonson had in mind was his attempt to amend men's manners by representing, for the first time on the English stage, "deedes and language such as men doe use," but another and not unrelated part of his innovation was his effort to fashion a new and self-conscious relationship with his audience.

Every Man Out begins with a lengthy induction in which Asper

[14] See W. David Kay, "The Shaping of Jonson's Career," *MP*, LXVII (1970), 229–31.

carefully explains Jonson's conception of humor and prepares the audience for the peculiar properties of satirical comedy. He also assigns Cordatus and Mitis their roles as chorus:

> I leave you two, as censors, to sit here:
> Observe what I present, and liberally
> Speake your opinions, upon every *Scene*,
> As it shall passe the view of these spectators.
>   (ll. 153–56)

In the course of the play Cordatus and Mitis express their opinions with a vengeance, interrupting and commenting upon the action literally dozens of times, occasionally at great length. The purpose of their comments is explicitly instructive, but less to improve the spectators' morals than to help them understand and accept the author's dramaturgy itself. At one point Mitis remarks, "mary, you shall give mee leave to make objections," and Cordatus answers: "O, what else? it's the speciall intent of the author, you should doe so: for thereby others (that are present) may be well satisfied, who happily would object the same you do" (II.iii.303–09). Mitis is thus the audience's surrogate and Cordatus is Jonson's, and the two maintain a dialogue which corresponds to the dialogue between the play and the audience.

Plays with inductions and choral commentaries were not unusual in the 1590s:[15] *The Spanish Tragedy* and *The Taming of the Shrew* are only two of the more famous among many examples. In *The Spanish Tragedy* Revenge is clearly analogous to the author of a play and plays Cordatus to the Ghost's Mitis, thereby helping the audience to accept the action and remain detached from it at the same time. But the choral paraphenalia of *The Spanish Tragedy* does not, as it does in *Every Man Out*, make us acutely and constantly aware of the workings of the play world and of its creator (Kyd himself, as opposed to Revenge). Kyd's play has something approximating a continuous story, into which we are deliberately drawn, and the bifocality of our response (partly involved like the Ghost, partly detached like Revenge) provides a means by which we may experience as well as understand the ironies of earthly and supernatural justice which it is the play's object to explore. Indeed, the chorus in *The Spanish Tragedy* develops more autonomy for the play world, not less, and would seem to have made it possible for subsequent revenge plays to become less obtrusively self-conscious and to incorporate comments or commentators within the contexts of self-contained actions.

[15] See C. R. Baskervill, *English Elements in Jonson's Early Comedy* (Austin, Tex., 1911), pp. 146–49; and Herford and Simpson, IX, 406–08.

In *Every Man Out*, on the other hand, there is no continuous story to engage our interest, and no self-contained action. Jonson absolutely insists that we pay at least as much attention to what he is doing as to what his characters are doing. Cordatus and Mitis are ubiquitous. Their dialogue is interspersed throughout the action and is used not only to make explicit comments upon the action but also to keep the audience at a distance from it. Moreover, Jonson includes two characters within the action itself, Macilente and Carlo Buffone, whose function it is to comment upon other characters, and they also contribute to keeping us at a distance, since we tend to apprehend the other characters through their eyes. They themselves, of course, we view through the eyes of Cordatus and Mitis. The end result of this proliferation of perspectives is that we are and must be aware of the play world not primarily as an image of the larger stage of life, but as the process and product of the playwright's art.

In some respects Jonson probably did not intend this. Certainly part of the purpose of his critical consciousness was to create a more immediate relationship with his audience and a drama of greater verisimilitude and "realism" than seemed possible to him with dramatic forms that were then available in the public theater. In a passage anticipating the more celebrated attack upon romantic stage conventions in the 1616 prologue to *Every Man in His Humour*, Mitis objects to Cordatus: "That the argument of his *Comoedie* might have beene of some other nature, as of a duke to be in love with a countesse, and that countesse to bee in love with the dukes sonne, and the sonne to love the ladies waiting maid: some such crosse wooing, with a clowne to their servingman, better then to be thus neere, and familiarly allied to the time." Cordatus answers with a medieval definition of comedy, an "*Imitatio vitae, Speculum consuetudinis, Imago veritatis*; a thing throughout pleasant, and ridiculous, and accommodated to the correction of manners" (III.vi. 195–201, 206–09). But the paradox is that the romantic comedy of crosswooing is more immediate and absorbing to an audience than Jonson's familiar actions, localized in time and place, for one of the most persistent and curious results of seventeenth-century theatrical attempts to become more realistic is that the attempts often call attention to their own artifice. So it is with the machinery of the court masque, and later with Restoration moveable scenery, which was designed to be seen *as it moved*,[16] and so it is with Jonson's often laborious engines for the amendment of men's manners.

In *Every Man Out* this awareness of artifice for the most part turns in upon itself. The play often gives the impression of being about the

---

[16] See Richard Southern, *Changeable Scenery* (London, 1952), pp. 17–176.

artistic problems which Jonson had set himself to define and solve rather than about the characters and their humours. In *Cynthia's Revels*, however, his next comical satire, Jonson begins to exploit dramatic self-consciousness more organically and in ways that were to have significance in later Jacobean drama. Like *Every Man Out*, *Cynthia's Revels* has an induction and commentators, but in *Cynthia's Revels* the commentators are partially absorbed into the action. Mercury and Cupid are disguised as human beings and participate in the action, but they are also gods whose supernatural power and knowledge permit them to make constant comments upon the behavior of the people around them. They thus stand naturally both within the action and outside of it, and their comments provide a perspective on the action which is at the same time part of the action. Jonson also develops perspectives through Crites' commentaries, through the general disposition of the play to stress symbolic, if not allegorical, characterizations and actions, and through the child actors who first performed the play. Unlike *Every Man Out*, *Cynthia's Revels* was presented at a private theater by a children's company, and the spectacle of children playing adults gave Jonson, as it helped give all writers for the children's companies, a built-in emphasis upon the artificiality of the play world itself and an intrinsic means of manipulating the audience's sense of distance from the stage.

All of these factors together—the dual roles of Mercury and Cupid, Crites' commentary, the considerable overt symbolism, and the children's aping of adults—create a theatrical structure which is manifestly self-conscious without, like *Every Man Out*, being altogether involuted. *Cynthia's Revels* sustains more momentum of action than the earlier play, directs more of our attention to that action, and demonstrates a greater capacity to integrate and make capital of its devices of detachment for the purposes of satire. The commentaries and the explicit allegorical episodes, such as the swooning of Argurion, provide obvious means by which we may understand and judge the affectations and vices of the characters. More subtle and significant is the use of our consciousness of the play world to dramatize how the characters, because of their vices or affectations, are really "actors," impelled and imprisoned by the roles which their humours have defined for them. "We acte our mimicke trickes," Crites remarks,

> with that free license,
> That lust, that pleasure, that securitie,
> As if we practiz'd in a paste-boord case,
> And no one saw the motion, but the motion;
>   (I.v.61–64)

and elsewhere he makes a catalogue of satiric characters explicitly in terms of the roles they play and the scenes in which they act (III.iii.iv). Many of the episodes in the play show fools coaching gulls how to "act" properly, Amorphus with Asotus (III.v), for example, and the effect of the play as a whole depends upon our apprehension of the action of all the gulls as in reality no more than the motion of puppets. Children act adults who behave like children; actors act human beings who behave like actors.[17]

What led Jonson to create so self-conscious a play world is hard to establish. One of the reasons or causes may be personal. As his critical harangues and his frequent diatribes against his audience demonstrate, he was exceptionally self-centered, and his egoism is necessarily reflected in the kind of relationship he establishes with his audience. Moreover, whether or not he was an anal erotic, as Edmund Wilson claims,[18] he certainly reveals a costiveness of artistic temperament in his consuming interest in the processes of his own creation.

But there are factors in Jonson's theatrical self-consciousness which are clearly not personal and which affected dramatists who did not possess his temperament. One is the demands of satire. Satire depends upon an awareness of the discrepancy between what is and what should be or between what characters profess and what they are. In Renaissance formal satire this awareness was created primarily by a rather schizo-phrenic satiric persona who combined within himself the roles both of *vir bonus* and satyr, the one trustworthy, homiletic, detached, the other impassioned and involved in the vice he castigated.[19] In the very early satirical comedies of the seventeenth century these constituents are dramatized separately, with railing and vituperative satyr figures within the action and disinterested, moral commentators outside of it.[20] Pre-cisely because the commentators insistently make explicit what may be only implicit in formal satire, their eventual effect is to italicize the audience's distance from the action and characters. Inevitably also, like Mitis and Cordatus or Mercury and Cupid, they call considerable at-tention to the art of the play. In later Jacobean works, tragedies as well as tragicomedies and comedies, the satiric persona of formal satire is partially reconstituted in the figure of a satiric intriguer who is both an agent and critic of the action, and the more obtrusive effects of the earlier commentators are modified, but even in these plays satiric com-ment, however expressed, carries with it a necessary degree of detach-

[17] John J. Enck makes this point in *Jonson and the Comic Truth* (Madison, Wis., 1957), p. 60.

[18] "Morose Ben Jonson," *The Triple Thinkers* (New York, 1948).

[19] See Kernan, *The Cankered Muse*.

[20] See O. J. Campbell, *Comicall Satyre*.

ment and self-awareness. The malcontents in Marston and Webster and the intriguers in Jonson are all highly self-conscious characters.

Allied to the effect of the satiric function upon Jonson's plays is the effect of the child actors. Though he inaugurated the genre of comical satire in the public theater, he wrote *Cynthia's Revels* and *The Poetaster* for the private theater, and it was in the private theater, as Harbage has shown, that the form was developed and exploited. The effect of the children's companies and of the particular audiences of the coterie theaters upon the plays performed there is problematic, but certain consequences seem likely. The private theater audience was more wealthy and better educated than the public theater audience, and therefore probably more interested in sophisticated drama.[21] Correspondingly, boys and men had different acting capabilities. Child actors were more suited to less than serious subjects (though they did act tragedy): normally they could not sustain a long romantic part (Shakespeare's heroines notwithstanding), and normally also a continuous story developing strong emotional entanglements was beyond their natural scope. They were good at repartee and wit, and their childishness itself probably called attention to the artifice of their acting and of the actions in which they were involved.[22] All of these characteristics, the limitations and the assets, are evident in Jonson's development of satirical comedy, as well as in the plays of all dramatists for the boys' companies. Jonson, in *Cynthia's Revels*, seems content to exploit the stylization of the childrens' acting without straining or exaggerating it: he does not call upon them for sustained emotional developments or relationships, and he certainly does not give them romantic parts. Marston, as we shall see, was clearly more disposed to use romance material and to highlight the discrepancy between the boys and the adult roles they played, but in doing so he exploited the boys' peculiar capabilities quite as much as Jonson. Both, in different ways, were creating a drama in which the childishness of the boys played a central role.

Another strand in Jonson's satirical comedy, which figures importantly in his own later plays as well as in the works of other Jacobean dramatists, Middleton preeminently, is the influence of the morality play. Satirical comedy may well have arisen at least partly as a response to contemporary social and economic conditions, but as in almost all

[21] See Introduction, note 3 above, and especially Armstrong, "The Audience of the Elizabethan Private Theaters." Interesting material on the nature of coterie audiences may also be found in Philip J. Finkelpearl, *John Marston of the Middle Temple* (Cambridge, Mass., 1969).

[22] See Introduction, note 3 above, and especially Shapiro, "Children's Troupes." See also Anthony Caputi, *John Marston, Satirist* (Ithaca, N.Y., 1961), pp. 80–116; and G. K. Hunter, *John Lyly* (Cambridge, Mass., 1962), pp. 89–114.

satire, the nature of the response was essentially reactionary, both in method and substance. The morality play, accordingly, provided not only the norms of precapitalist, communal, and Christian behavior which satiric dramatists could use to expose contemporary vice, but also a dramatic structure which would itself embody such norms. It is no accident that moralities were part of the repertory of the private theaters in the late nineties and early 1600s and that they were commonly performed at the Inns of Court which served as nurseries for both coterie playwrights and their audiences.[23]

The whole stress of Jonson's theory of humours, it is worth remembering, is upon a moral rather than psychological conception of character and behavior,[24] and this is especially clear in *Cynthia's Revels*. The third boy's summary of the plot in the induction reads like a synopsis of a morality. The characters are described as "vices," and are named after their dominant moral traits, as for example, "PHILAUTIA, or *selfe-love*, a court-ladie," "ASOTUS, or the *prodigall*," "ARGURION, *monie*." Their actions are described by the boy in similarly emblematic terms: "There CUPID strikes *monie* in love with the *prodigall*"; "they conclude upon a *Masque*, the device of which is . . . that each of these vices, being to appear before CYNTHIA, would seeme other then indeed they are: and therefore assume the most neighbouring vertues as their masking habites" (ll. 56, 68–69, 73, 76, 98–102). The play itself bears out the allegorical promise of the boy's description. The characters often behave like personifications, and some of their actions, like the swooning of Argurion and the disguise of the vices as their opposing virtues, are derived from traditional morality play devices.

The morality influence, moreover, is even more penetrating than the personifications and emblematic actions at first suggest, for in significant respects Cupid, Mercury, and Crites function like a combination of the Vice figure and the presenter of the morality plays. Crites is throughout a mixture of the satiric persona of formal satire and the presenter, constantly exposing and excoriating the vices and follies of the other characters; and Cupid and Mercury, though their purposes are more gracious than those of the Vice and though they are not allegorical extensions of the characters, as the Vice is, nevertheless have a similar theatrical omnipotence in the way in which they cast the characters in their roles, manipulate them, and comment upon how they act. The effect of Crites, Cupid, and Mercury together is to create a sense of ironic and satiric

---

[23] See Finkelpearl, *John Marston*, p. 119. *Every Man Out*, significantly, is itself dedicated "To the Noblest Nourceries of Humanity, and Liberty, in the Kingdome: The Innes of Court."

[24] See James Redwine, "Beyond Psychology: The Moral Basis of Jonson's Theory of Humour Characterization, *ELH*, XXVIII (1961), 316–34.

dispassion in the audience which can be considered comparable to the effect of the allegorical structure of a morality play.

The influence of the morality play, upon Jonson as upon other Elizabethan and Jacobean dramatists, can of course be exaggerated and lead to reductive criticism. Jonson is quite obviously not a medieval playwright, and much of the vitality of his plays, even of *Cynthia's Revels*, results from the way in which his characters break out of their schemata and assert an individuality which we never find in morality drama. But the morality still deserves emphasis in studying Jonson, not only because of its many overt resemblances to his plays, but also and more important because of the analogies it offers to the kind of relationship between the audience and the play which he himself sought. A self-conscious theatricalism is an important ingredient of morality plays, especially of the later ones in which the Vice predominates: in this later morality drama the whole play is in a sense the Vice's play, the characters both roles which he casts and directs and roles which are universally assumed by human beings; and the effect of the drama is evolved through an interplay between the audience's latent and conscious senses that the whole of the world is such a stage.[25] In Jonson's early plays the metaphysical dimension is much narrower: we apprehend the actors acting in Cupid's "*comoedie* . . . that would not be lost for a kingdome" (*Cynthia's Revels*, V.x.6–7), but we are far more likely to refer them to Jonson and his stage than to the Creator and His. But despite this difference—a great one, and one which should not be minimized—the dramatic methods of Jonson and morality drama remain significantly similar: both are satiric and both dramatize their satire through the creation of a heavily ironic sense of detachment from the characters who are "acting out" their moral humours. Both habitually have commentators and surrogate playwrights; both, though in different ways, make capital of the audience's consciousness of the stage and of playmaking itself. In a sense we can see Jonson as deliberately adapting the morality to a new theatrical epistemology—which is what he himself said he was doing later in his career. In the second Intermeane of *The Staple of Newes* (1626), when Tatle complains that there is no "Fiend" in the play and that he will "not give a rush for a *Vice*, that has not a wooden dagger to snap at every body he meetes," Mirth answers, "That was the old way, Gossip, when *Iniquity* came in like *Hokos Pokos*, in a Juglers jerkin, with false skirts, like the *Knave* of

[25] Here, as elsewhere in this book, I am indebted to the analysis of the development of the Vice figure and morality play by Bernard Spivack, *Shakespeare and the Allegory of Evil* (New York, 1958). See also David Bevington, *From "Mankind" to Marlowe* (Cambridge, Mass., 1962); and T. W. Craik, *The Tudor Interlude* (Leicester, 1958).

Clubs! but now they are attir'd like men and women o' the time, the *Vices*, male and female! *Prodigality* like a young heyre, and his *Mistresse* Money (whose favours he scatters like counters) prank't up like a prime *Lady*, the *Infanta of Mines*" (ll. 11–20).

How much the "new" way changes the morality until it is another thing is problematic. The change is obviously greatest in Jonson's successful comedies, though it has been argued that *Volpone* and *The Alchemist* are also related to morality play patterns, in particular those of the estates moralities of the later sixteenth century.[26] In the comical satires, as well as in *The Staple of Newes* itself, the bones of the morality play show through more unquestionably, but even in the comical satires it is worth stressing that the morality offered Jonson an analogy more than a direct source, an analogy which permitted him to develop his own dramatic temperament and to capitalize upon the contemporary theatrical milieu. Jonson had a strong satiric bias which he sought to dramatize through unromantic comedy; he was theatrically self-conscious, as apparently was his private theater audience; and his boy actors were finely suited to convey both the satire and the self-consciousness. The morality plays offered dramatic precedents for these tendencies. They are, in a sense, comical satires themselves (they are certainly unromantic) and the dramatic devices through which they realize their comedies of evil—Vice playmakers, presenters, commentators, discontinuous actions—are comparable to those in Jonson. Even though it may be just, therefore, to stress the role of formal satire in Jonson's creation of the genre of satiric comedy, the morality tradition offers perhaps the best means of understanding how Jonson translated this satire into drama.

"Comicall satyre" thus is composed of diverse elements and is at once traditional and highly innovative. Jonson drew upon old dramatic patterns to shape a drama calculated to satisfy the demands both of a fadish coterie theater and of his own strong artistic interests. A common denominator of these factors, I have been suggesting, is a pervasive theatrical self-consciousness which seeks at once to involve the spectator in the playwright's art and to oblige him to stand apart and observe it. One critic has argued that even in his drama Jonson was always moving toward that simultaneously intimate and artificial relationship with his audience which is exemplified so perfectly in his masques.[27] In *Every Man Out* and *Cynthia's Revels* this kind of relationship is trans-

---

[26] Alan C. Dessen, "*The Alchemist*: Jonson's 'Estates' Play," *Renaissance Drama*, ed. S. Schoenbaum, VII (1964), 35–54; and "*Volpone* and Late Morality Tradition," *MLQ*, XXV (1964), 383–99.

[27] Stephen Orgel, *The Jonsonian Masque* (Cambridge, Mass., 1965), pp. 198–200.

parent and provides the solution in which are suspended the diversities of satire, morality, child acting, and Jonson's own artistic ego. In a later masterpiece like *Volpone*, conscious theatricalism and the elements from which it is spawned are more subtly and brilliantly modulated, but are no less central: Volpone and Mosca, as many critics have observed, are playmakers as well as actors all the time, and we respond to their plots and roles (and to an extent to those of the gulls as well) both as moral emblems of human vice and folly and as splendid theatrical conceits. Volpone and Mosca are above all consummate actors and it is primarily as such that we react to them and to the plays within the play which they write and direct. The mountebank scene, for example, is a perfect union of the dynamics of human folly and the dynamics of theatrical illusion, Jonson's two consuming interests: the habitual self-deception of human beings merges indistinguishably with both the conscious and unconscious deceptions of the actor and the theater, for Volpone is implicated in the folly which he exploits and is himself a projection of the audience before whom he acts. He plays a mountebank and is one at the same time, and he plays both roles for us as well as for the audience on stage.

Jonson never used the consciousness of theater to more spacious and elegant purpose, and part of the reason for this spaciousness may be that *Volpone* was written for the public theater and could draw upon that theater's traditionally resonant sense of *theatrum mundi*. In any event, with the exception of Shakespeare and Middleton, Jonson's Jacobean contemporaries and successors usually cultivated a consciousness of the stage in the more limited (and often more limiting) ways of the comical satires, and not coincidentally, these dramatists were either largely or totally oriented towards the private theater. Marston, whom we shall now consider, wrote for the private theater exclusively.

II

Marston

AMONG Marston's earliest plays are the two-part drama consisting of *Antonio and Mellida* and *Antonio's Revenge*, written around 1599, and *The Malcontent*, which was probably written in 1603. The earlier plays seem in many respects analogous to Jonson's comical satires, whereas *The Malcontent*, which was entered in the Stationers' Register as a "Tragicomoedia," appears to be responding to the stimulus of Guarini, but all three form a coherent sequence and indicate both the potentialities and dangers of the theatrical style which was evolving in the private theaters in the early years of the century.

In common with most plays written for the children's companies, *Antonio and Mellida* and *Antonio's Revenge* are satiric and extremely self-conscious. In each there are several characters making running comments on the action and on each other: *Antonio and Mellida* begins with an induction which discusses the roles of the play in some detail, both plays are interspersed with songs, and both are filled with comments and actions which italicize the play world itself. The result is drama of exceptional preciosity. In Act IV of *Antonio and Mellida*, for example, after a series of disguises, mishaps, and escapes, all equally improbable, the hero and heroine discover each other and start speaking in Italian, to the amazement of an onlooking page:

> Ant. *Spavento dell mio core dolce Mellida,*
> *Di grava morte restoro vero dolce Mellida*
> *Celesta salvatrice sovrana Mellida*
> *Del mio sperar; trofeo vero Mellida.*
>
> Mel. *Diletta & soave anima mia Antonio*
> *Godevole belezza cortese Antonio.*
> *Signior mio & virginal amore bell' Antonio*
> *Gusto delli mei sensi, car' Antonio.*
>
> Ant. *O suamisce il cor in un soave baccio,*
> Mel. *Murone i sensi nel desiato dessio;*
> Ant. *Nel Cielo puo lesser belta pia chiara?*
> Mel. *Nel mondo pol esser belta pia chiara?*
> Ant. *Dammi un baccio da quella bocca beata,*
> *Bassiammi, coglier l'aura odorata*
> *Che in sua neggia in quello dolce labra.*

Mel.　*Dammi pimpero del tuo gradit' amore*
Che bea me, cosempiterno honore,
Cosi, cosi mi converra morir.[1]
Good sweet, scout ore the marsh: for my heart trembls
At every little breath that strikes my eare.
When thou returnest: and ile discourse
How I deceiv'd the Court: then thou shall tell
How thou escapt'st the watch: weele point our speech
With amorous kissing, kissing cõmaes, and even suck
The liquid breath from out each others lips.

Ant.　Dul clod, no man but such sweete favour clips.
I goe, and yet my panting blood perswades me stay.
Turne coward in her sight? away, away.

[*Luc.*]　I thinke confusion of *Babell* is falne upon these lovers, that they change their language; but I feare mee, my master having but fained the person of a woman, hath got their unfained imperfection, and is growne double tongu'd; as for *Mellida*, she were no woman, if shee coulde not yeelde strange language. But howsoever, if I should sit in judgement, tis an errour easier to be pardoned by the auditors, then excused by the authours; and yet some private respect may rebate the edge of the keener censure.[2]

(IV.i.182–219)

A comparable scene occurs in *Antonio's Revenge* when, after an enumeration of some of the horrors he has either accomplished or hopes to accomplish, the villain Piero summons the fool Balurdo:

[1] *Ant.* Terror of my heart, sweet Mellida, true medicine against sad death, sweet Mellida, heavenly savior, Mellida, sovereign of my hope, true trophy, Mellida.

Mel. Antonio, my chosen and delightful soul, courteous Antonio, delightful in beauty, fair Antonio, my lord and love of my virginity, dear Antonio, food for my affections.

Ant. O dissolve my heart in a sweet kiss.

Mel. Let the senses die in fulfilled desire.

Ant. Can there be a purer good in heaven?

Mel. Can there be a purer good on earth?

Ant. Give me a kiss from your blessed mouth. Let me gather up the perfumed air which nests up there in these sweet lips.

Mel. Give me the empire of thy consenting love, which blesses me, with an eternal honor, for true, thus it is fit that I should die.

The translation is G. K. Hunter's, *Antonio and Mellida*, Regents Renaissance Drama Series (Lincoln, Neb., 1965), pp. 58–59.

[2] References to Marston's plays are to the texts of the first editions: *The History of Antonio and Mellida. The First Part* (London, 1602); *Antonio's Revenge. The Second Part* (London, 1602); and *The Malcontent. Augmented by Marston. With the Additions played by the Kings Majesties servants. Written by John Webster* (London, 1604). Act, scene, and line references are to *The Works of John Marston*, ed. A. H. Bullen, 3 vols. (London, 1887).

Pie.   *Andrugio* rots;
    Antonio lives: umh: how long? ha, ha; how long?
    Antonio packt hence, Ile his mother wed,
    Then cleare my daughter of supposed lust,
    Wed her to *Florence* heire. O excellent.
    Venice, Genoa, Florence at my becke,
    At *Piero's* nod. *Balurdo*, ô ho.
    O, twill be rare, all unsuspected donne.
    I have been nurst in blood, and still have suckt
    The steeme of reeking gore. *Balurdo*, ho.
                            Enter Balurdo with a beard, halfe of, halfe on.

Ba. When my beard is on, most noble prince, when my beard is on.

Pie. Why, what dost thou with a beard?

Ba. In truth, one tolde me that my wit was balde, & that a Meremaide was halfe fish, and halfe [flesh]; and therefore to speake wisely, like one of your counsell, as indeede it hath pleased you to make me, not onely being a foole, of your counsell, but also to make me of your counsell, being a foole; If my wit be bald, and a Mermaid be halfe fish and halfe cunger, then I must be forced to conclude—the tyring man hath not glewd on my beard halfe fast enough. Gods bores, it wil not stick to fal off.

Pie. Dost thou know what thou has spoken all this while?

Ba. O Lord Duke, I would be sorie of that. Many men can utter that which, no man, but themselves can conceive: but I thanke a good wit, I have the gift to speake that which neither any man els, nor my selfe understands.

Pie. Thou art wise. He that speaks he knows not what, shal never sin against his own conscience: go to, thou art wise.

                                                    (II.i.11–40)

Both of these scenes are typical, and the knowledge that they were performed by children in the atmosphere of a private theater seems to lead fairly naturally to the conclusion, suggested by several critics,[3] that the plays are essentially burlesque entertainments. "Seriously fantasticall" is the phrase Marston himself uses to describe them. Recently, however, other critics, notably G. K. Hunter and Philip J. Finkelpearl, have been disposed to interpret this phrase differently and to find much more of interest in the plays. Hunter argues that parody is not an end in itself and that both dramas capitalize upon consciousness of theater in a manner not unlike Pirandello's. He suggests that the discontinuity of action in Marston's plays is an expression of a similar discontinuity of human experience, and that the apparent parodic betrayal of his art is an expression of an essential self-betrayal of human behavior. "*An-*

[3] See Anthony Caputi, *John Marston, Satirist*, pp. 80–116; and R. A. Foakes, "John Marston's Fantastical Plays," *PQ*, XLI (1962), 229–39.

tonio and Mellida," for example, "asks us to see the matter of court
intrigue as at once passionately serious and absurdly pointless; and
there is no good reason for supposing that Marston thought one of these
viewpoints more basic than the other." Hunter sees such a perspective
in both Marston's comedy and tragedy and argues that all of the features
of his dramaturgy which might seem frivolous or defective are func-
tional and organic. "The statuesque scenes, the simplified characterization, the emotion on stilts" all collaborate to produce an "operatic style"
which is a perfect expression of the absurdist vision which Marston
wishes to communicate.[4] Finkelpearl interprets the plays similarly.
Antonio and Mellida, he argues, depicts "a sordid world governed by
an absurd, prideful, and unjust ruler. The protagonists respond by
uttering cries of anguish and by making theatrical, impotent gestures
of defiance. Marston rigorously controls the action and the characters
so that we see a comic vision: sensitive, melancholic, would-be trage-
dians mouthing Seneca and, absurdly, gaining a fragile success through
the benevolence of their bitterest enemy." *Antonio's Revenge* places
the same characters "in a genre where their rhetoric and actions will
be congruent." Antonio, who in the earlier play had been treated largely
satirically, an effeminate Romeo in a capriciously benevolent world,
now becomes a corrupt Hamlet in a world where there is no special
providence and in which, as Marston remarks in the induction, we are
required to see "what men must be." Finkelpearl also suggests, like
Hunter, that the modern theater of absurdity and cruelty should help
us understand the dramaturgy of these plays, and he stresses particularly
the nonmimetic, "Mannerist" techniques of *Antonio's Revenge.*[5]

Both critics succeed in demonstrating that these plays have coherent
enough intellectual intentions, but what remains arguable is how well
these intentions are realized in dramatic form. Part of the problem is
that Marston lacks a sense of proportion. Just as the various styles of
speech in the plays tend to be exaggerated and uncoordinated—as Jonson was only the first to notice—so are the scenes which they compose.
Antonio and Mellida courting each other in Italian no doubt parody
Petrarchan and Shakespearian lovers, but the exchange is so discrete and
extended that the final impression it leaves is of sheer self-indulgence.
The same is true of the "wisdom" developed in the scene between Piero
and the half-bearded Balurdo and of the effect of a host of other scenes
in both plays, as a few more examples should suffice to show. There is
an episode, for example, in *Antonio and Mellida* in which Antonio and
his father Andrugio meet after each has given up the other as dead. It

---

[4] Introduction to Regents Drama Series edition of *Antonio and Mellida,* pp. xvii,
xxi.

[5] *John Marston,* pp. 148–49, 150, 160–61.

is a stock scene of romance (both plays are littered with recognition scenes), and Marston's parody of it is intellectually consistent, but it is exaggerated to a point that forces us to respond primarily to the dramatist's own archness. Andrugio has just been declaiming upon stoic fortitude when his servant mentions the name of his long lost son. Andrugio immediately begins a passionate lament for Antonio. Antonio, who has been lying on the ground nearby (lamenting, in his turn, the loss of Mellida) hears him:

Ant. Antonio?
And. I, eccho, I; I meane *Antonio.*
Ant. Antonio, who meanes *Antonio?*
And. Where art? what art? knowst thou *Antonio?*
Ant. Yes
And. Lives hee?
Ant. No.
And. Where lies hee deade?
Ant. Here.
And. Where?
Ant. Here
And. Art thou *Antonio?*
Ant. I thinke I am.
And. Dost thou but think. What, dost not know thy selfe?
Ant. He is a foole that thinks he knowes himselfe.
(IV.i.91–99)

Eventually, after several more lines like these, they embrace.

There is a similar strain of burlesque and exaggeration in scenes which are ostensibly serious as well as those which are meant to be funny. Piero, in *Antonio and Mellida*, hearing of the elopement of his daughter, is clearly meant to be comic in his anger:

stay, runne to the gates, stop the gundolets, let none passe the marsh, doe all at once. *Antonio?* his head, his head. Keep you the Court, the rest stand still, or runne, or goe, or shoute, or search, or scud, or call, or hang, or doe doe doe, su su su, something: I know not who who who, what I do do do, nor who who who, where I am.

> *O trista traditriche, rea, ribalda fortuna,*
> *Negando mi vindetta mi causa fera morte.*
> (III.ii.179–87)

This may, as Hunter and Finkelpearl suggest, be an inventive exploration of the speech of a man under stress, but it sounds very close to what we would now call "camp."[6] Comparable effects in *Antonio's Revenge*,

[6] For some interesting analogies, see Jacob Brackman, "The Put-On," *New Yorker* (June 24, 1967), pp. 34–73. Finkelpearl himself, it seems to me, speaks in

in scenes which at least initially look as if they should be taken seriously,
seem even more difficult to justify. Here, for example, is Antonio's
speech of premonition early in the play:

> I tell you bloods
> My spirit's heavie, and the juyce of life
> Creepes slowly through my stifned arteries.
> Last sleep, my sense was steep'd in horrid dreames:
> Three parts of night were swallow'd in the gulfe
> Of ravenous time, when to my slumbring powers
> Two meager ghosts made apparition.
>
> .   .   .   .   .
>
> Three times I gasp't at shades:
> And thrice, deluded by erroneous sense,
> I forc't my thoughts make stand; when loe, I op't
> A large bay window, through which the night
> Struck terror to my soule. The verge of heaven
> Was ringd with flames, and all the upper vault
> Thick lac't with flakes of fire; in midst whereof
> A blazing Comet shot his threatning traine
> Just on my face. Viewing these prodigies,
> I bow'd my naked knee and pierc't the starre,
> With an outfacing eye; pronouncing thus:
> *Deus imperat astris.* At which, my nose straight bled;
> Then doubl'd I my word, so slunke to bed.
>
> (I.ii.102–8, 114–26)

The burlesque of the public theater revenge conventions is clear enough.
What is less certain is if there is anything more. The immediate response
to the speech by the clown *cum* theatrical critic Balurdo would seem to
indicate not:

Verely, Sir *Gefferey* had a monstrous strange dream the last night. For
mee thought I dreamt I was asleepe, and me thought the ground yaun'd
and belkt up the abhominable ghost of a misshapen *Simile*, with two ugly
Pages; the one called master, even as going before; and the other *Mounser*,
even so following after; whilst *Signior Simile* stalked most prodigiously in
the midst. At which I bewrayed the fearefulnesse of my nature, and being
readie to forsake the fortresse of my wit, start up, called for a cleane shirt,
eate a messe of broth, and with that I awakt.

(I.ii.127–37)

---

terms suggestive of "camp" when he describes the revels at the Inns of Court which
he argues lie behind Marston's plays (*John Marston*, pp. 32–44).

The net effect of such scenes is not so much to destroy the thought of these plays as to displace it. Marston's continual juxtapositions of Stoic ideals and Senecan reality, theatrical postures and actual performance, tend to be exploited rather than explored. They provide obvious occasions for a simultaneous display of the passion of the characters and the conceit of their author, and because they are extreme as well as predictable, their intellectual point becomes subordinated to an appreciation of their contrivance. Moreover, since Marston habitually represents the impotence of his characters by having them assume histrionic stances, the theatrical self-consciousness of the plays is exceptionally acute.

Judging by the testimony of the dramatists who wrote for them, coterie audiences had to be continually flattered into watching the plays they had presumably come to watch and assured that they would not have to suspend their sophistication. This kind of detachment, like many other circumstances of the theater, could be a creative challenge for a dramatist, as it was for other Jacobean playwrights, as well as for Marston himself in *The Malcontent*, but in these early plays Marston's response tends to be defensive.[7] It is most significant, for example, that for all the theatricalism of the plays, their usual attitude towards the theater is patronizing, if not contemptuous. Characters habitually make sardonic references to actors, stigmatizing "apish action, player-like," refusing to "swell like a Tragedian, in forced passion of affected straines," confessing that "all this while I ha' but plaid a part, / Like to some boy, that actes a Tragedie, / Speakes burly words, and raves out passion" (*Antonio's Revenge* I.ii.318; II.ii.109–10; IV.ii.70–72). It is true that these statements have a didactic point, the world of action being consistently associated with the world of acting in order to suggest the futility of man's fate, but the association is at once mechanical and sterile. Nowhere in these plays do we find, as we do in Jacobean coterie dramatists like Jonson and Middleton as well as modern playwrights like Pirandello, the kind of enterprising exploration of the nature of theatrical illusion that makes the comparison between the world and the stage an imaginative metaphor rather than a simple

---

[7] John Peter, *Complaint and Satire in Early English Literature* (Oxford, 1956), pp. 157–58, cites an interesting anecdote about Marston recorded in Manningham's *Diary*: "Jo. Marstone the last Christmas he daunt with Alderman Moses wives daughter, a Spaniard borne. Fell into a strang commendacion of hir witt and beauty. When he had done, shee thought to pay him home, and told him that she though[t] he was a poet. 'Tis true,' said he, 'for poets faine and lie, and soe did I when I commended your beauty, for you are exceeding foule.' " The anecdote is certainly suggestive, though as Arnold Davenport, *The Poems of John Marston* (Liverpool, 1961), pp. 25–27, points out, Peter's attempt to argue from this episode as well as from the works that Marston was neurotic, is to miss the point.

analogy. The sense of the theater in Marston is used primarily destruc-
tively, to cut down his characters and deflate their actions. The result,
paradoxically, is that he not only undermines the very medium he employs, but makes it appear to be feeding upon itself.

The case is conspicuously and instructively different with *The Malcontent*, which, under the stimulus of Guarini, manages to turn many
of the same tendencies into positive and disciplined effects. There are
a number of specific borrowings from the 1602 translation of *The
Pastor Fido* in the play,[8] but these are less important than its overall
response to Guarini's controlling tragicomic ideas.

The Malcontent, in some respects, is a continuation and amalgam of
Antonio and Mellida and *Antonio's Revenge*, combining similar tragic
and comic "crosses" in a single play. In any case, it presents the same
kind of sordid Senecan world as the earlier plays and the same kinds
of theatrical self-consciousness and operatic exaggeration. The Induction to the pirated version which was presented at the Globe by the
King's Men in 1604, as well as other additions, make these concerns
virtually explicit for the public theater audience, but they are evident
enough in the Blackfriars original. As in the earlier plays, the intrigue
in *The Malcontent* is intricate and peripetetic, providing occasions for
a gamut of emotional displays and at the same time calling attention to
its own artifice. At one point early in the play, for example, the villainous Mendoza delivers an ecstatic encomium upon "sweete women,
most sweete Ladies, nay Angells," (I.i.340ff.) and barely a few minutes
later, when his mistress rejects him (as we knew she would), he has an
equally passionate diatribe against "Women? nay furies" (I.ii.85ff.).
The patently excessive rhetoric of each speech, as well as the deliberate
counterpointing, creates an awareness of design which not only cauter-
izes Mendoza's villainous threats, but also compels us to pay as much
attention to how he delivers his lines as to what they express.

In this instance we watch Mendoza unconsciously play a role, but
there is also an extraordinary amount of conscious role-playing in *The
Malcontent* whose inevitable effect is similarly to make us aware of
actors acting. A curious feature of these acts is that though we know
the characters are pretending, we see that they are in fact also expressing
real feelings. Thus, for example, when Mendoza rants to Pietro the
Duke about the Duchess's wantoness, we know that the Duchess has
been Mendoza's mistress and that what he is really castigating is her
unfaithfulness to himself. Similarly, late in the play, Pietro disguises
himself as a witness to his own suicide and relates his death speech, a

---

[8] See Bernard Harris, ed., *The Malcontent*, The New Mermaids (London, 1967),
pp. xxv–xxvii, 18, 30, 35, 45–46, 58, and 80.

passionate and deeply felt aria about the impossibility of living with the knowledge of his wife's adultery. The speech is an act—we have been party to its rehearsal—and yet at the same time it expresses Pietro's actual feelings.

The same kind of role-playing, conscious and unconscious, characterizes *Antonio and Mellida* and *Antonio's Revenge*—there is, for example, a similar death speech related by Antonio, disguised as an Amazon, to Mellida—but in these early plays it is usually simply reductive, an indiscriminate, if not cynical, assumption that life is no better than a play. In *The Malcontent*, on the other hand, role-playing and the self-consciousness it breeds both in the characters and the audience truly become a mode of vision, an organized and sympathetic way both of conceiving and representing human behavior. The chief instrument of this achievement is the characterization of Malevole-Altofront, whose supreme and dominating role-playing crystallizes the whole of the play. Altofront is a dispossessed Duke who, though bitter, seeks not only to reclaim his rule but to regenerate his enemies. In doing this he assumes the role of a satiric commentator, the malcontent Malevole. Through his occasional undisguised speeches to Celso (as well as through some stage directions indicating him "shifting" his speech to different people) we learn quite early that he is playing a role and that the role does not really express his intentions, but since it does express his predicament and feelings we can never entirely believe or disbelieve his vituperative rhetoric. Early in the play Pietro describes Malevole in terms which were traditional for the malcontent figure: "th' Elements struggle within him; his own soule is at variance within her selfe" (I.i.35–36). By endowing his malcontent with another persona, however, Marston makes this description doubly true—true of Malevole alone and of the relationship between him and Altofront. The result is a character of considerable but convincing ambivalence. We are compelled always to respond not to one man but to an amalgam of two, Malevole and Altofront, an amalgam which is at once a disjunction, an act, and an expression of the real thing, for Malevole is also a projection of Altofront, a part of him. As a consequence we respond to all of Malevole-Altofront's actions and speeches, except perhaps those to Celso, in a very complex way.

This complexity spreads out to the whole play once Malevole's beneficent control (and creation) of the action is assured. No matter what happens our reactions are necessarily qualified, if not determined, by the ambiguities of his role, so that in any given situation we are moved by what a character feels at the same time that we are aware that the character is an actor in a play within a play directed by an actor. The effect is richly illustrated in the scene, late in the play, in which Malevole-Altofront is sent to solicit his own wife, Maria, for Mendoza.

He is disguised, so that she cannot recognize him, and though obviously tortured by his role, he nevertheless plays it to the hilt:

Mully, he that loves thee, is a Duke, *Mendoza*, he will maintaine thee royally, love thee ardently, defend thee powerfully, marry thee sumptuously, & keep thee in despite of *Rosiclere* or *Donzel del Phoebo*: thers jewels, if thou wilt, so; if not, so.

Turning to the Captain of the Guard, Maria answers:

> Captaine, for Gods sake save poore wretchedness
> From tyranny of lustfull insolence:
> Inforce me in [t]he deepest dungeon dwell
> Rather then heere; heere round about is hell.
> O my dear'st *Altofront*, where ere thou breath,
> Let my soul sincke into the shades beneath,
> Before I staine thine honor, this thou hast;
> And long as I can die, I will live chaste.
>
> (V.ii.112–24)

Beyond its simple dramatic irony, what is important about this scene is that the hell Maria sees about her is both there and not there, just as we are both moved and not moved by her speech. The scene is staged, and though she does not know it, Altofront stands before her guaranteeing her ultimate safety; but the staging itself is hellish both for Malevole and her, and their pain is no less real because we can be partly dispassionate about it. Detachment in this case is an organic expression of complexities of feeling and situation, not a retreat from them.

Immediately after this scene Malevole is revolted by the role he feels compelled to sustain, but acknowledges its necessity: "ô God, how loathsome this toying is to me, that a duke should be forc'd to foole it: well, *Stultorum plena sunt omnia*, better play the foole Lord, then be the foole Lord." (V.ii.139–42). This comment reveals not only the primary motive of his characterization but its unifying function in the play as a whole. After about the end of Act II, *The Malcontent* is Malevole's play —he is its central intelligence and the author and director of its action— and as we come to accept his own role-playing, with all its attendant ambivalences, as a natural expression of the society he inhabits, so we come to accept the role-playing of others. With Malevole as both a cause and effect, all the theatrically self-conscious devices of Marston's earlier plays suddenly become articulated into a whole which makes them expressive. Malevole-Altofront holds in suspension within himself the various disjunctions of emotion and attitude which in the previous plays simply co-existed mechanically, and his operatic behavior becomes an intelligible emblem of the world to which he responds as well as of his own character.

Malevole-Altofront contributes to the coherence of this world in another crucial way, for he acts to a limited extent as a providential agent who is, and makes us, aware that he is fulfilling a tragicomic design. Throughout the play he alludes to the inevitability of fate and the perpetual turns of Fortune's wheel, and the lesson which he draws from his observations is that though it is "hopelesse to strive with fate" (I.i.240), a man can and must "temporize"—he uses the word twice (I.i.240; IV.ii.178)—since though the mighty fall, the lowly also rise. Thus, he insists to Celso very early in the play that " '*Hees resolute who can no lower sinke*' " (I.i.255); he warns Mendoza that " '*subtile Hell dooth flatter vice,/ Mounts him aloft, and makes him seeme to flie,/ ... onely, that from height he might dead fall*' " (II.ii.52–53, 56); he quotes Seneca's "*Neminem servum non ex regibus, neminem regem non ex servis esse oriundum*," adding that "only busie fortune towses, and the provident chances blends them together; ile give you a similie; Did you ere see a wel with two buckets, whilst one comes up ful to be emptied, another goes downe empty to be filled; such is the state of all humanitie" (III.i.271–77); and, finally, he assures Pietro that given the hellish vicissitudes of the world " '*A stedie quickenes is the soule of state*' " (III.ii.79).

The accent of these comments is traditionally pessimistic, but their constructive stress, evident especially in the notion that "Hees resolute who can no lower sinke," is what actually forms the basis of Malevole's actions in the play. A "virtuous Machiavellian,"[9] he never deserts his belief that the world is diabolically mutable, but he also perceives the whole of the circle which Fortune's wheel describes and the Providence of God which informs it: "*For no disastrous chance can ever move him,/ That leaveth nothing but a God above him*" (V.ii.285–86), he tells Celso; and this perception leads to regenerative impulses both within himself and in his behavior towards others. Altofront, though an identity partly independent of Malevole, is also bred like a phoenix in the ashes of Malevole's satiric indictments, for Altofront's humiliation, which is both assumed and real, gives him the insight and resolution to temporize and rise. The same kind of homeopathic cure is the motive behind Malevole's treatment of others, particularly Pietro, the man who stole his throne. Throughout the play Malevole probes Pietro's wounds

[9] The phrase is Finkelpearl's; for his entire argument about *The Malcontent*, see *John Marston*, pp. 178–94. See also G. K. Hunter, "English Folly and Italian Vice," in *Jacobean Theatre*, eds. Brown and Harris (London, 1960), pp. 84–111.

and contrives situations which are designed to exacerbate his pain and
to humble him. The process reaches its climax when Pietro's resulting
self-abnegation turns to contrition. During the scene in which this occurs, in a speech much like the Duke's to Claudio at the beginning of
Act III in *Measure for Measure*, Malevole tells Pietro:

> thinke this: This earth is the only grave and *Golgotha* wherein all things
> that live must rot: tis but the draught wherein the heavenly bodies dis-
> charge their corruption, the very muckhill on which the sublunarie orbes cast
> their excrements: man is the slime of this dongue-pit, and Princes are the
> governors of these men; for, for our soules, they are as free as Emperours, all
> of one peece; there goes but a paire of sheeres betwixt an Emperor and the
> sonne of a bagge-piper, onely the dying, dressing, pressing, glossing, makes
> the difference: now what arte thou like to loose?
>
> > *A Jaylers office to keepe men in bonds,*
> > *Whilst toyle and treason, all lifes good confounds.*
> >   (IV.ii.141–52)

Pietro's immediate response is to renounce his regency and in "true
contrition" to dedicate himself to holiness and the restoration of Altofront to his throne. At this point Malevole "undisguiseth himselfe" (for
the first time) and exclaims:

> Who doubts of providence
> That sees this change, a heartie faith to all:
> *He needes must rise, can no lower fall,*
> For still impetuous vicissitude
> Towzeth the world, then let no maze intrude
> Upon your spirits: wonder not I rise,
> *For who can sincke, that close can temporize?*
>   (IV.ii.172–78)

This is a rather worldly interpretation of Providence, but it serves
nevertheless to give *The Malcontent* a recognizable and constructive
tragicomic shape. Partly by virtue of it, the play has a center and the
capacity to make the characteristically troublesome features of Marston's
earlier dramaturgy more manageable. His vitriolic satire becomes a
form of homeopathis, the combination of absurdity and seriousness is
genuinely expressive, and theatrical self-consciousness does not simply
turn in upon itself. The self-regarding style of *The Malcontent* helps
dramatize a condition of human behavior which is evident in Malevole-
Altofront's own intricate role-playing, as well as in his manipulation of
others, and works consistently to keep us conscious both of the disjunc-
tive elements of the action and of the ultimately beneficent resolution

towards which they are moving. The stimulus for this achievement was almost certainly *The Pastor Fido*, from which Marston borrows heavily in the play. The example of Guarini's tragicomedy enabled him, for the first time in his dramatic career, to express his artistic sensibility in an effective form.

III

Beaumont and Fletcher

INDEBTED to both Guarini and Jonson, the theatrical style which Beaumont and Fletcher and their collaborators created at once encompasses and dilutes the polarities of romance and satire. Fletcher's actual definition of tragicomedy reads very much like Guarini's, from which it was clearly borrowed. "A tragie-comedie," he wrote in the preface to *The Faithful Shepherdess* (1608), "is not so called in respect of mirth and killing, but in respect it wants deaths, which is inough to make it no tragedie, yet brings some neere it, which is inough to make it no comedie: which must be a representation of familiar people, with such kinde of trouble as no life be questioned; so that a God is as lawful in this as in a tragedie, and meane people as in a comedy."[1] As in the case of Guarini, among the natural consequences of such a conception of a play is a self-conscious emphasis upon plot and style, and like Guarini, Beaumont and Fletcher have an exceptional interest in declamatory rhetoric—in their case directly derived from Senecan declamations[2]—and in copious and intricate plots organized less on causal than on spatial principles. Where their practice diverges significantly from Guarini's is in their lack of interest in an overall providential pattern. *The Pastor Fido*, as we have observed, is designed to culminate in a recognition scene which verifies the comic dispensation of the art both of the Creator and the dramatist; *The Faithful Shepherdess*, as all of Beaumont and Fletcher's subsequent plays, though nominally devoted to providential precepts, in fact makes little use of them to organize the action.[3]

Beaumont and Fletcher's debt to satirical comedy leads in a similar

---

[1] References to Beaumont and Fletcher's plays are to the texts of the first editions: *The Faithful Shepherdess* (London, ca. 1609); *The Maid's Tragedy* (London, 1619); *The Scornful Lady* (London, 1616); and *The Humorous Lieutenant* (London, 1647). Act, scene, and line references for these plays are to *The Works of Francis Beaumont and John Fletcher*, Variorum edition, gen. ed. A. H. Bullen, 4 vols. (London, 1904-12). References to the text and act, scene, and line numbers of *Philaster* are to *The Dramatic Works in the Beaumont and Fletcher Canon*, gen. ed. Fredson Bowers, I (Cambridge, 1966).

[2] See Eugene M. Waith, *The Pattern of Tragicomedy in Beaumont and Fletcher*, pp. 86–98.

[3] See ibid., pp. 5-11.

direction. As Eugene Waith has shown,[4] many of the most notable characteristics of Fletcherian tragicomedy have roots in Jonson's and Marston's practice: the atmosphere of evil, Protean characterizations, extreme and schematic oppositions of emotions as well as characters, moral dilemmas that are acute but disengaging, and kaleidoscopic plots. In Jonson and Marston, however, these features are at least intended to serve the purposes of satire. In Beaumont and Fletcher, though a detritus of satire remains, there is no comparable sense of purpose, and the same characteristics receive an abstracted and more formal emphasis. As with the debt to Guarini, the net result is frequently less meaning and more art, plays with effects of unusual virtuosity but also unusual self-consciousness.

This stress upon artifice for its own sake is confirmed by the testimony of Beaumont and Fletcher's contemporaries. James Shirley, who was perhaps their best critic as well as a devoted disciple, wrote in the preface to the 1647 collection of their works:

You may here find passions raised to that excellent pitch and by such insinuating degrees that you shall not chuse but consent, & go along with them, finding your self at last grown insensibly the very same person you read, and then stand admiring the subtile Trackes of your engagement. Fall on a Scene of love and you will never believe the writers could have the least roome left in their soules for another passion, peruse a Scene of manly Rage, and you would sweare they cannot be exprest by the same hands, but both are so excellently wrought, you must confesse none, but the same hands, could worke them.

Would thy Melancholy have a cure? thou shalt laugh at *Democritus* himselfe, and but reading one piece of this *Comick* variety, finde thy exalted fancie in Elizium; And when thou art sick of this cure, (for excesse of delight may too much dilate thy *soule*) thou shalt meete almost in every leafe a soft purling passion or *spring* of sorrow so powerfully wrought high by the teares of innocence, and *wronged Lovers*, it shall perswade thy eyes to weepe into the streame, and yet smile when they contribute to their owne ruines.[5]

Here is theatrical plenty, and Shirley's description reveals not only the variety of passions which Beaumont and Fletcher were able to exploit, but also the unusual sophistication of their effects. The insistence in this description upon the recognition of artifice goes beyond the traditional capacity of Elizabethan drama to be simultaneously realistic and symbolic, to make us aware of the analogies between the stage and the

[4] Ibid., pp. 62–70.
[5] *Comedies and Tragedies Written by Francis Beaumont and John Fletcher Gentlemen* (London, 1647), sig. A3v.

world, and to involve us in the action and at the same time to keep us
detached enough to make judgments about it. Shirley places decisive
stress upon detachment, upon the constant recognition of the play as a
play, as the work of an artist. It is a matter of emphasis, but a crucial
one. To Shirley, as to virtually all of their contemporaries, the excellence
of Beaumont and Fletcher rested not simply in their ability to capture
an audience, but in their capacity to do so with an elegance that was
self-revealing.[6]

Perhaps the most transparent example of this artfulness occurs in
Philaster, in the scene which gave the play its subtitle, "Love lies a
Bleeding." Philaster has come upon Arathusa in the woods. She is at-
tended by Bellario, his own page. Unaware that Bellario is Euphrasia
in disguise (and in love with him), Philaster misinterprets the meeting
and launches a passionate diatribe against faithlessness:

> Let me love lightning, let me be embrac't
> And kist by Scorpions, or adore the eyes
> Of Basalisks, rather then trust the tongues
> Of hell-bred women. Some good god looke downe
> And shrinke these veines up; sticke me here a stone
> Lasting to ages, in the memory
> Of this damned act.
>
> (IV.v.27–33)

At a word from Arathusa, however, he quickly reverses his mood:

> I have done;
> Forgive my passion: Not the calmed sea,
> When *Eolus* locks up his windy brood,
> Is lesse disturb'd then I; I'le make you know't.
>
> (IV.v.41–44)

In a replay of a scene in *The Faithful Shepherdess*, he then offers his
sword to Arathusa and Bellario to kill him. Both of course refuse and
Philaster, in a counterturn, prepares to use the sword to "performe a

---

[6] See, e.g., the commendatory poems to the 1647 folio by Robert Herrick, sig.
b2; Robert Stapylton, sig. a4v; John Denham, sig. bv; John Earle, sigs. c3v–[c4];
William Cartwright, sigs. dv–d2v; G. Hills, sig. fv; Alexander Brome, sig [f3];
and Richard Brome, sig. g. Virtually all the commendatory poems to the folio, and
there are over 50 pages of them, stress Beaumont and Fletcher's conscious artistry.
Only one writer, "T. Palmer of Ch. Ch. Oxon," sig. f2v, discusses their capacity to
engage an audience so deeply that it will lose sight of that artistry (*"How didst
thou sway the Theatre! . . . we could not stir away | Untill the Epilogue told us
'twas a Play*), but the compliment is largely a decorative conceit, and Palmer spends
most of his poem praising Beaumont and Fletcher's dramatic wit.

peece of Justice" upon Arathusa. At that moment, however, a "countrey fellow" enters and the situation becomes quite remarkable:

Countrey Fellow. There's a Courtier with his sword drawne, by this hand
           upon a woman, I thinke.
Philaster.   Are you at peace?
Arathusa.   With heaven and earth.
Philaster.   May they divide thy soule and body.
                                      Philaster *wounds her.*
Countrey Fellow. Hold dastard, strike a woman! th'art a craven: I warrant
           thee, thou wouldst be loth to play halfe a dozen venies at
           wasters with a good fellow for a broken head.
Philaster.   Leave us good friend.
Arathusa.   What ill-bred man art thou, to intrude thy selfe
           Upon our private sports, our recreations.
Countrey Fellow. God uds me, I understand you not; but I know the rogue
           has hurt you.
Philaster.   Persue thy owne affaires; it will be ill
           To multiply blood upon my head, which thou
           Wilt force me to.
Countrey Fellow. I know not your rethoricke, but I can lay it on if you
           touch the woman.
                                          They fight.

Philaster is wounded and, hearing the court party approaching, runs off. The country fellow demands a kiss from Arathusa, and only after he learns that she is a princess does he lose his fine uncouth country poise. His last words are: "If I get cleare of this, I'le goe to see no more gay sights" (IV.v.80–97, 142–43).

The scene was evidently very popular—it is not only referred to in the subtitle of the play but pictured in a woodcut on the title page of the first edition (1620)—and it constitutes a paradigm of Fletcherian dramaturgy. It is entirely contrived to allow for striking if not sensational contrasts of emotion. The whole situation is false and improbable, and since we know it is, we consciously follow the ebb and flow of Philaster's passion, responding to his diatribes and laments as declamatory exercises. The intervention of the country fellow italicizes the wholly self-regarding theatricality of the scene even further. In the peculiar dialectic of Fletcherian dramaturgy the country fellow would seem to represent a popular ideal of honor which Philaster at that point lacks,[7] but at the same time his emphatic outlandishness serves to qualify any serious apprehensions we might develop about Philaster and Arathusa and

---

[7] See Peter Davison, "The Serious Concerns of *Philaster*," *ELH*, XXX (1963), pp. 1–15.

thus to preserve the mood of tragicomedy. His honorable uncouthness is finally an urbane joke, a conceit which paradoxically insulates the boundaries of Beaumont and Fletcher's world of gay sights and protects its private sports and recreations. His appearance not only assures us that any wound Arathusa receives has been made with a pasteboard sword, but absolutely compels us to become conscious of the preciousness of the entire scene.

The scene is an extreme instance, but it is nonetheless typical of the play as well as of much of Beaumont and Fletcher's subsequent work. Their later tragicomedies and tragedies are more carefully modulated, more versatile, more elegant, but not fundamentally different in kind. They rarely employ so stark a device to define and emphasize their theatrical conceits: the juxtapositions of characters and scenes, or of contrasting emotions within a character, are more integrated with one another and more graceful; but their essential purposes and effects remain the same as *Philaster's*. *The Maid's Tragedy*, the play which is usually acknowledged as their masterpiece and which certainly exhibits their resources to great effect, is a case in point, and an especially important one, I think, both because a few critics have been inclined to see a different kind of accomplishment in it and because an understanding of the effect of Beaumont and Fletcher's characteristic tragicomic patterning upon an ostensive tragedy is very suggestive in interpreting plays of other seventeenth-century dramatists.

Three scenes in *The Maid's Tragedy* were especially celebrated by contemporary audiences and may stand as typical examples of its dramaturgy: Amintor's and Evadne's wedding night (II.i), Aspatia mourning with her maids (II.ii), and the quarrel between Amintor and Melantius (III.ii).[8] The first scene, the wedding night, is a typical Fletcherian dramatic conceit—an outrageous and multiple inversion of conventional expectations. The scene is set in a bed-chamber and begins, traditionally enough, with a maid making bawdy comments which apparently embarrass Evadne. A pathetic melody is counterpointed to the bawdy by the presence of Aspatia, the maid whom Amintor was supposed to marry until the King ordered him to marry Evadne. Amintor meets Aspatia outside the chamber and asks Evadne to come to bed: "Come, come, my love, / And let us loose our selves to one another" (II.i.149–50). But she protests, and after a protracted discussion Amintor assures her that she could preserve her maidenhead one more night by other means if she wished. She answers, "A maidenhead *Amintor* at my yeares" (ll. 198–99). The scene continues with a number of similarly

---

[8] Abraham Wright, for example, singles out these three scenes as the best in the play; quoted in Kirsch, "A Caroline Commentary on the Drama," p. 259.

sensational turns. Evadne swears that she will never sleep with him, not because she is coy but because she does already "enjoy the best" of men, with whom she has "sworne to stand or die" (ll. 301–02). Amintor furiously demands to know who the man is so that he may "cut his body into motes" (l. 304). Evadne obligingly informs him that "tis the King" (l. 309), and that the King had ordered their marriage to mask his own affair with her. Amintor responds to his cuckoldom by turning royalist:

> Oh thou has nam'd a word that wipes away
> All thoughts revengefull, in that sacred word,
> The King, there lies a terror, what fraile man
> Dares lift his hand against it, let the Gods
> Speake to him when they please: till when let us
> Suffer, and waite.
> (ll. 313–18)

In a final turn, Amintor begs Evadne that for the benefit of his honor they may pretend before the court to have fulfilled the rites of a wedding night. She agrees and he coaches her on how she should behave in front of morning visitors:

> And prethee smile upon me when they come,
> And seeme to toy as if thou hadst been pleas'd
> With what I did. . . .
> Come let us practise, and as wantonly
> As ever longing bride and bridegroome met,
> Lets laugh and enter here.
> (ll. 360–62, 63–65)

The scene, as John F. Danby has shown,[9] is like a dramatized metaphysical conceit, a rich exploration of progressively inverted Petrarchan images culminating in a demand that the lover either literally kill himself for his mistress or serve her as a pandar and a cuckold (which he does). In dramatizing this conceit, however, the scene exhibits many of the usual trademarks of Fletcherian tragicomedy: the constant peripeties, the discontinuous characterization (Evadne appears alternately as virgin and whore), the systematic betrayal of conventional expectations; and despite the apparent burden of "metaphysical meaning," the emphasis is still upon display and expertise. The scene's outrageousness, like that of the country fellow's in *Philaster*, points finally to itself, at once insulating the action from belief as well as ridicule and italicizing

---

[9] *Poets on Fortune's Hill* (London, 1952), pp. 188–93.

its artifice. It is entirely appropriate that the final turn should show us
two actors preparing themselves to "act" the "scene" which we had
expected them to act in the first place.

Immediately following this episode, and in counterpoint to it, is the
scene showing Aspatia in mourning with her maids. It has no witty
turns and its pace is deliberately measured, designed to depict a static
tableau of Aspatia's grief. Typically, we are conscious of the scene as a
tableau since one of Aspatia's maids is embroidering a picture of the
wronged Ariadne on the island of Naxos, and Aspatia, applying the
scene to herself, tells the maid how a grief-stricken woman should really
appear:

> Fie, you have mist it there *Antiphila*,
> You are much mistaken wench:
> These colours are not dull and pale enough,
> To show a soule so full of miserie
> As this poore Ladies was, doe it by me,
> Doe it againe, by me the lost *Aspatia*,
> And you will find all true but the wilde Iland,
> Suppose I stand upon the Sea breach now
> Mine armes thus, and mine haire blowne with the wind,
> Wilde as the place she was in, let all about me
> Be teares of my story, doe my face
> If thou hadst ever feeling of a sorrow,
> Thus, thus, *Antiphila* make me looke good girle
> Like sorrowes mount, and the trees about me,
> Let them be dry and leaveless, let the rocks
> Groane with continuall surges, and behind me,
> Make all a desolation, see, see wenches,
> A miserable life of this poore picture.
>
> (II.ii.61–78)

Charles Lamb remarked in *Specimens of English Dramatic Poets*
that, in contrast to Shakespeare, the finest scenes in Fletcher are "slow
and languid. [Their] motion is circular, not progressive. Each line re-
solves on itself in a sort of separate orbit. They do not join into one another like a running hand. Every step that we go we are stopped to admire some single object, like walking in beautiful scenery with a
guide."[10] This description captures perfectly the statuesque and self-
regarding quality of the scene with Aspatia. The setting of that scene is
the island of grief which Aspatia at once describes and represents. She
is the guide to the scenery as well as its emblem, and because she is
both, the pathos she elicits calls for a sophisticated response: we are

[10] (London, 1808), p. 403.

meant to feel her grief, but even more to admire it as a virtuoso example of passionate theater portraiture. There are comparable portraits everywhere in Fletcher's plays, though those which occur in scenes marked by witty turns of speech and action are more changeable and less sustained. The distinction of Aspatia's scene is its static emphasis, an emphasis that became increasingly important in the plays of Webster and Ford.

The third of the scenes in *The Maid's Tragedy* that were especially admired in the seventeenth century is the one dealing with the quarrel between Amintor and Melantius (III.ii). The scene is particularly important because it reveals so transparently the dynamics of the Fletcherian patterning of action. It is composed entirely of the kinds of turns and counterturns of love, honor, friendship, &c. which were to become the staples of Caroline and Restoration drama. The scene begins with Melantius questioning Amintor about the strangeness of his behavior. Amintor refuses to explain until Melantius threatens to dissolve their friendship, at which point Amintor confesses that Evadne, who is Melantius' sister,

> Is much to blame,
> And to the King has given her honour up,
> And lives in whoredome with him.
> (III.ii.128–30)

Melantius responds by drawing his sword:

> shall the name of friend
> Blot all our family, and stick the brand
> Of whore upon my sister unreveng'd.
> (ll. 139–41)

Amintor, however, welcomes death as a relief from his sorrows and in any case refuses to draw upon his friend, but after Melantius calls him a coward, he does draw his sword. Melantius immediately reflects that "The name of friend, is more then familie, / Or all the world besides" (ll. 172–73), and sheaths his sword. When Amintor does likewise, they are reconciled; but Melantius threatens to kill the King, and Amintor then draws his sword, both because he is opposed to regicide and because he does not wish his cuckoldom to become known. Melantius draws his sword, and after further discussion, they both sheath their weapons and their dance finally ends.

Rymer's comment upon this scene in *The Tragedies of the Last Age* was that "When a Sword is once drawn in Tragedy, the Scabbard may be thrown away."[11] The remark is myopic but revealing, for Beaumont and Fletcher are clearly not interested in tragic decorum. In the quarrel between Brutus and Cassius which was probably the model for their scene the turns of action and sentiment grow out of the characters of the two men, their evolving relationship with one another, and their particular situation. Amintor and Melantius are not comparably defined, nor is their quarrel. What characters they have are largely postulates for the turns and counterturns in which they are engaged, for theirs is a choreographic abstraction of the Shakespearian scene, a *pas de deux* in which movements of swords and declamations upon friendship have equal meaning. The substance of their quarrel *is* its design.

John F. Danby has seen in such designs and in the kind of scenes that elicit them "not only literary entertainment, but literature aware of itself as a symptom rather than a reflection of the dangerous reality surrounding it—aware of a world that cannot be trusted, and in which the mind is forced back upon itself to make a world of its own, by belief, or resolve, or art."[12] Danby argues that for Beaumont and Fletcher this reality is composed of absolutes—among them, Honor, Kingship and Petrarchan Love—"which have to be chosen among and which it is nonsense to choose among." He contends further that Beaumont and Fletcher are interested not in assessing any of these absolutes separately but in opposing them, for their "best work" and "main interest" lie "in the conflict of the absolutes and the contortions it imposes upon human nature."[13] On the basis of these assumptions he concludes that *The Maid's Tragedy*, in particular, is a searching expression of the disorientation of values in Jacobean society, conveyed through exceptionally subtle characterizations. Evadne, for example, "a study in radical perversity ... is more compelling than Lady Macbeth, and more subtle"; Melantius, though the soul of honour, is essentially a representative of "the simplifying madness of war"; and Aspatia "represents that large and immovable continent of the traditional morality from which the 'wild island' of Beaumont's dramatic world detaches itself."[14]

There is a great deal in these arguments which deserves attention. Danby's consideration of the relationship of Beaumont and Fletcher to their social milieu certainly helps explain their extraordinary popularity and his particular analyses of Fletcherian wit are often acute. For a num-

---

[11] *Critical Essays of the Seventeenth Century,* ed. Joel Spingarn (Oxford, 1908), II, 204.

[12] *Poets on Fortune's Hill,* p. 167.

[13] Ibid., p. 166.

[14] Ibid., pp. 193, 205. A similar analysis of the characters of *The Maid's Tragedy* may be found in Howard Norland's introduction to his edition of the play (Lincoln, Neb., 1968), pp. xi–xxii.

ber of reasons, however, it is difficult to accept his general assessment of Beaumont and Fletcher's intrinsic achievement. In the first place, it is a fallacy common in criticism of the plays which he discusses to see a theatrical style which is self-conscious and which can be entirely self-regarding as necessarily a reflection of Jacobean *angst*. Danby may well be correct in his assumptions about the sociological sources of Fletcherian drama, but the critical issue is whether these sources are meaningful parts of the plays themselves. James's court and the general decay of Elizabethan standards may have encouraged the enshrinement of absolutes "which have to be chosen among and which it is nonsense to choose among," but in the actual scenes in *The Maid's Tragedy* and *Philaster* in which protagonists make such choices, the real emphasis is upon the contrivance with which the choices are posed and disposed rather than upon what they represent. It is difficult, and we are not intended, to take either the absolutes or the protagonists very seriously. The choices are indeed empty of meaning, and not because they are the expression of an empty or disoriented society, but because the alternatives they pose are essentially rhetorical counters in a theatrical display. The quarrel scene between Amintor and Melantius asserts absolutely nothing about Kingship or Honor, either negatively or positively. Inherited ideas of kingship or honor are adverted to solely to provide opportunities for debate and turns of action. In this respect the old judgment, held by both Coleridge and Eliot, that Beaumont and Fletcher's plays are parasitic and without inner meaning, seems just.

Nor do Beaumont and Fletcher, either in *The Maid's Tragedy* or *Philaster*, really explore the stress which the conflicts they contrive place upon human nature, as Danby also claims, for, psychologically considered, the characters in these plays simply do not have sufficient substance to explore. They are all primarily elements in a spatial design and they follow completely from the design, not the design from them. They are accordingly portrayed with radical discontinuities, capable of Protean change, like Evadne, or with consistent but stereotyped humours, like Melantius (honor) or Aspatia (grief), which are equally in the service of a peripetetic action. The true contortions of Beaumont and Fletcher's situations in these plays are thus rhetorical and theatrical, and their ultimate stress is less upon the nature of the participants than upon the artifice which employs them.

A case can and should be made for the possibilities of such artifice, but on different grounds and with different plays, for it is in their comedies, it seems to me, rather than in works like *The Maid's Tragedy,* that Beaumont and Fletcher's real achievement lies. Plays like *The Scornful Lady, The Humourous Lieutenant,* and *The Wild Goose Chase,* apparently more trivial than the tragicomedies and tragedies, are

at the same time less guilty of trifling with ideas and need neither ex-
cuses nor footnotes about baroque mentality to explain them. They
explain and justify themselves, and the reason is that as with the Restoration comedies of manners of which they are precursors, as indeed with
all good plays, their artifice and their subjects give substance to each
other.

   The Scornful Lady was written by Beaumont and Fletcher in col-
laboration and shows Beaumont's influence in its satiric emphasis and
in its strong humours characterizations. *The Humourous Lieutenant*,
written by Fletcher alone, mixes comedy with threats of tragedy, while
The Wild Goose Chase, also an unaided Fletcherian work, is more
strictly a comedy of intrigue. At the heart of all three plays, however,
is a sexual combat in which one lover wittily and persistently foils the
attempts of another to make him or her submit to love and marriage. In
The Scornful Lady the Lady of the title resists Elder Loveless's efforts to
make her acknowledge her love, and the bulk of the play consists of
their intrigues against one another. In *The Humourous Lieutenant*
Celia toys contrarily with the true passion of her lover and frustrates the
villainous passion of his father. In *The Wild Goose Chase* three witty
couples spawn intrigues and counter-intrigues: in two of them it is the
women who have the "brave spirit" of contention, in the third it is
Mirabel, the man. The theme of wit combat is not in itself new—Shakespeare, among others, had represented it with obvious mastery in *Much
Ado About Nothing*—but Beaumont and Fletcher make it peculiarly
their own because the peripeties of action and feeling, the declamations,
the intricate intrigues, the discontinuous, Protean characterizations, in
short, the characteristics which are bred by their tragicomic style, are
also and precisely the characteristics which express the comic manners
of a witty couple.

   The Scornful Lady depicts these manners with perhaps the greatest
insight. The Lady—she has no other name—is represented as a woman
whose humour does not permit her to submit to a man, even one she
loves. In a series of encounters she alternately spurns and appears to
favor her lovers while they correspondingly praise or vilify her. The
most remarkable of these scenes is the one which eventually leads her
to relent. Elder Loveless, who has already been duped and rejected by
her, comes to her house to mock her and boast of his escape from
bondage:

Neither doe I thinke there can bee such a fellow found i' th' world, to be in
love with such a froward woman: if there bee such, th'are madde, *Jove* comfort um. Now you have all, and I as new a man, as light, & spirited, that I
feel my selfe clean through another creature. O' tis brave to be ones owne

man. I can see you now as I would see a Picture, sit all day by you, and never kiss your hand, heare you sing, and never fall backward; but with as set a temper as I would heare a Fidler, rise and thanke you.

(IV.i.224–34)

At first unmoved by such diatribes, the Lady after a while appears to be deeply affected. She asks to speak "a little private" with him and accuses him of perjuring himself; he laughs at her "set speech," her "fine *Exordium*"; she kisses his hand and swoons into the arms of her sister, who has just entered the room. Predictably, Elder Loveless then reverses course completely, railing upon himself as passionately as he had upon her and vowing that it was only a trick, that he always has loved her:

for sooner shall you know a generall ruine, then my faith broken. Doe not doubt this Mistres: for by my life I cannot live without you. Come, come, you shall not greeve, rather be angry, and heape infliction on me: I wil suffer.   (ll. 275–79)

Suffer indeed he does as the Lady, her sister, and her maid proceed to break into laughter and the Lady tells him he has been finely fooled. He then rails upon her in earnest:

I know you will recant and sue to me, but save that labour: I'le rather love a Fever and continual thirst, rather contract my youthe to drinke, and safer dote upon quarrells, or take a drawne whore from an Hospital, that time, diseases, and *Mercury* had eaten, then to be drawne to love you.

(ll. 366–73)

He flees and at precisely that moment, the Lady asks her servant Abigail to recall him: "I would be loth to anger him too much: what fine foolery is this in a woman, to use men most frowardly they love most?" Abigail agrees, remarking, "this is still your way, to love being absent, and when hee's with you, laugh at him and abuse him. There is another way if you could hit on't" (ll. 383–85, 392–94).

The scene is a perfect counterpart of the debate between Amintor and Melantius or the wedding night of Amintor and Evadne. Like them it consists of extreme turns and counterturns, of characters whose emotions oscillate violently, of declamations which are at once passionate and contrived. Like them also, it calls repeated attention to the artifice of its own construction. The difference is that whereas in *The Maid's Tragedy* the extreme discontinuities of character and the turns of passionate debate which are their consequence can be accepted only as theatrical conventions, in *The Scornful Lady* they represent credible human behavior. Elder Loveless's contortions are the reflection of a young man in love, while the artifices of the Lady are the expression of a woman who finds herself incapable of accepting not only the love of a man but the reality of her own feelings. Interacting with one another, the two form a pattern representing the dynamics of a recognizable human relationship. Their perversities, their posturings, conscious and otherwise, spring from something resembling psychological integrity. Thus the sophistication of our response to them enables us to appreciate both the artifice (theirs and the dramatists') of the ballet which they dance and the meaning behind it.

The Humourous Lieutenant, a full-blown tragicomedy, is less consistent and less penetrating than *The Scornful Lady*, but the portrait of its heroine Celia has some of the same virtues. Unlike the Lady, Celia is in part a romantic figure, very much in love with Demetrius and usually very willing to say so. But she also, like the Lady and indeed like most of Fletcher's women, has a brave streak in her, and it is this part of her character that is most prominent in the play. When Demetrius's father, King Antigonus, pursues her with lecherous designs while Demetrius is away fighting, alternately tempting and threatening her, she resists with a high spirit, declaiming satirically and at length on the corruption of courtiers and kings. Persuaded as much by her energy as her chastity, Antigonus eventually becomes her convert, praising the virtue which he had before suspected. At this point Demeterius comes home, and unaware of the full situation, suspects her himself. She then turns upon him: "he's jealous; / I must now play the knave with him, [though I] dye for't, / 'Tis in me nature" (IV.viii.54–56). A quarrel ensues in which she castigates him for his lack of faith and he contritely asks her forgiveness. Antigonus himself is obliged to command that she forgive him.

Celia swings between extremes of romance and satire which appear incompatible,[15] but her character, if not profound, is nevertheless of a piece. Her diatribes are the other side of the coin of her love, for she is motivated by love as much in the satiric condemnations of Antigonus's lust as in the criticism of Demetrius's faithlessness. The extremes through which she travels are thus plausible and though they are also exaggerated they still denote a coherence of feeling. She is indeed still capricious, but the caprice is clearly hers, not simply the dramatist's.

The Wild Goose Chase is less concerned with the psychology of its characters than either *The Scornful Lady* or *The Humourous Lieutenant*. Its emphasis is upon the spirit which they display and the con-

---

[15] Cf. Waith, *Pattern of Tragicomedy*, pp. 151–54, who argues that the two are incompatible and finally make Celia both improbable and insignificant as a character.

trasts they create rather than upon their motivations. Oriana pursues the witty and reluctant Mirabel, Pinac and Belleur chase the equally witty and reluctant sisters, Lillia-Bianca and Rosalura. Each group is in counterpoint to the others and within each the lovers continuously adopt opposing postures, some conscious, some not. Their *pas de deux* are symmetrically balanced and end only after the exhaustion of every contrast of every movement. Once again, however, stylization has a relation to content. Mirabel, Lillia-Bianca, and Rosalura (as well as Celia and the scornful Lady) look forward to the heroes and heroines of Restoration comedy. Like their descendants, they habitually don masks which reflect not only their pleasure in acting roles, but their need to do so in order to respond to the requirements of their personal relationships. Their wit, thus, expresses their sexual identity as well as their social grace, and the consciously elegant patterns which their courtships form at least begin to represent the nature of their society as well as the art of the dramatist.

It is no doubt curious that the pattern of tragicomedy which Beaumont and Fletcher crystallized should have produced less merit in the tragedies and tragicomedies themselves than in the comedies, but it is nonetheless true. Without either the vision of fortunate suffering which informs Shakespeare's dispassion or the moral clarity which informs Middleton's, the detachment and self-consciousness which Beaumont and Fletcher's style breeds turn in upon themselves when applied to a serious subject; and this was to be a most damaging legacy in seventeenth-century drama, affecting playwrights like Webster, Ford, and Dryden, as well as comparative hacks like Massinger and Shirley. In their tragicomedies and tragedies Beaumont and Fletcher's men in action are essentially formal devices, theatrical fragments, and no amount of special pleading can mend them or give them human dimension. It is only in some of their comic writing that Beaumont and Fletcher can truly be said to have held a mirror up to nature, and it is no accident that it was in this genre that they left their most enduring legacy to the repertory of the English stage. Congreve was born of many parents, but not least among them were Beaumont and Fletcher, who were the first, as Dryden saw, to represent "the conversation of gentlemen."

IV

Shakespeare

IT IS a kind of indecorum to associate Shakespeare with his contemporaries even the best of them, and for some critics it is still a heresy. Yet his life as well as his work suggest that he was a professional who was responsive to his theatrical environment, and the improprieties of criticism arise less from this responsiveness itself, both natural and inevitable for a repertory dramatist, than from the ways in which it has often been interpreted. It is obviously not necessary that analogies between Shakespeare and contemporary dramatists lead to reductive conclusions. Shakespeare may have been affected by the example of his colleagues without becoming like them. No doubt the final product therefore illustrates the uniqueness of his reaction to theatrical stimuli, but we should not for that reason ignore the stimuli. They are important and they can be extremely illuminating.

The argument that in the later part of his career Shakespeare was affected by the developments of the tragicomic and coterie drama that we have been discussing is especially persuasive. There is external evidence, notably the acquisition of Blackfriars by the King's Men in 1608,[1] but the best evidence comes from the plays themselves. We will focus particularly upon *All's Well That Ends Well* and *Cymbeline*. Both are representative, and they are curiously similar, especially in the kinds of difficulties they have posed for critics.

All's Well That Ends Well

Most critics of *All's Well That Ends Well* seem to be agreed that like the other problem comedies it suffers from an inability to unify or assimilate its own material.[2] The most obvious problem, as Johnson observed,[3] is Bertram. For virtually the whole of the play Bertram is, as

---

[1] See especially Bentley, "Shakespeare and the Blackfriars Theatre." Bentley confines his argument to the last plays; for a discussion of the possible effects of the private theater upon Shakespeare earlier in the 1600s, see Robert Kimbrough, *Shakespeare's "Troilus and Cressida" and its Setting* (Cambridge, Mass., 1964).

[2] See Joseph G. Price, *The Unfortunate Comedy. A Study of All's Well That Ends Well and its Critics* (Liverpool, 1968), especially pp. 87–109.

[3] "I cannot reconcile my heart to Bertram: a man noble without generosity, and

Parolles describes him, "a foolish idle boy, but for all that very ruttish" (IV.iii.207).[4] Shakespeare insists, as the source does not, upon his adolescent callowness, upon his lust, and upon his deceitfulness. His contemptuous response to Helena's suit is deliberately contrasted to that of the other young lords whom the King offers to her; his refusal to kiss her when they part is deliberately callous; and his letter outlining the tasks she must fulfill is gratuitously cruel: *"Till I have no wife I have nothing in France"* (III.ii.74). At the end, Bertram is fooled into happiness and tricked into redemption and is never more unattractive than at the very moment he is achieving both. He squirms and lies under Diana's accusations, betraying even the limited honor he has managed to gain on the battlefield.

That Helena should have to suffer such a man, and more, that she should choose to love him, are of course the real problems of the play and Shakespeare does not allow us to resolve them simply by treating them as conventions and thereby ignoring them. Helena is too warm, in her expression as in her conception, and too alert to her own predicament for us to be able to explain away the obvious disproportions between her and the apparent child to whom she aspires. Where he is merely a boy, she is a woman; where he is callow, she is sensitive; and where he is emotionally unprepared for love, she is its creature and its emblem. The painfulness of these dichotomies is continually forced upon our consciousness not only by the commentaries of characters like the King, Lafew, and the Countess, but by the responses of Helena herself. She is no Griselda, and her story is not one which such an analogue would explain. She feels too much, and we are a witness to those feelings. She may behave like her clever folk prototypes in eventually fulfilling the tasks which her husband commands of her, but she does not easily accommodate herself to the animus behind the commands—as she says, " 'Tis bitter" (III.ii.75)—nor can she easily forget the lust to which she had to submit in Florence:

> O strange men!
> That can such sweet use make of what they hate,
> When saucy trusting of the cozen'd thoughts

---

young without truth; who marries Helen as a coward, and leaves her as a profligate: when she is dead by his unkindness, sneaks home to a second marriage, is accused by a woman he has wronged, defends himself by falshood, and is dismissed to happiness." *Yale Johnson*, VII, ed. Arthur Sherbo (New Haven, 1968), 404.

[4] References to the texts and act, scene and line numbers of the plays of Shakespeare are to the Arden editions: *All's Well that Ends Well*, ed. G. K. Hunter (London, 1959); *Cymbeline*, ed. J. M. Nosworthy (London, 1955); and *The Winter's Tale*, ed. J. H. P. Pafford (London, 1963).

> Defiles the pitchy night; so lust doth play
> With what it loathes for that which is away.
>   (IV.iv.21–25)

The eventual result of such speeches and of the predicaments which give rise to them is a sense that Helena is abused not only by Bertram but by Shakespeare as well. She seems, at times, a creature from another kind of play, too richly endowed both for her husband and for the plot in which she is called upon to act.

There are, moreover, other symptoms in *All's Well* of a similar sense of disproportion and "strain."[5] Throughout the play, for example, there seems to be an opposition between realistic and romantic motives. Lavatch's "foul mouth'd" calumnies have a satiric bias which appears not merely to parody Helena's quest but to depreciate it. Parolles's characterization, though intelligible enough in morality play terms—he is the word where Helena is the deed of honor, Bertram's vice where she is the virtue—seems at odds with the expressive mode in which Helena herself exists, and the scenes of his exposure, in particular, have a dissonant and distinctly Jonsonian ring. The play as a whole raises moral issues—the nature of honor most especially—which seem both inadequately expressed and summarily resolved in the action itself. Like Helena's relationship to Bertram, the action and the ideas it contains appear disjoined, and never more so than in the play's ending. A theatrically self-indulgent *scène à faire*, the last scene, like its counterpart in *Measure for Measure*, appears not so much to resolve the intellectual and emotional issues of the play as to circumvent them.

The majority of critics have tried to cope with these problems, and others like them, by in effect emphasizing one element or impulse in the play at the expense of another. Thus, some have stressed the conventional romantic and folkloristic nature of Helena's difficulties, while others have insisted upon the considerable satire in the play and the intractability of much of its material to romantic treatment.[6] Precisely because each of these views is justified, however, neither is alone sufficient to establish an integrity for the play. Helena's tasks (and solutions) are no doubt conventional, but their tradition hardly explains the abrasive

[5] The word is G. K. Hunter's, in his introduction to the Arden edition of the play, p. xxix; most of the evidences of strain that I mention are discussed at length by Hunter.

[6] Cf., e.g., W. W. Lawrence, *Shakespeare's Problem Comedies* (London, 1931), pp. 43–79, who argues that Helena should be understood as a romantic heroine facing essentially conventional (and medieval) tasks, and Clifford Leech, "The Theme of Ambition in *All's Well*," *ELH*, XXI (1954), 17–29, who believes that Helena is tainted by ambition.

ways in which Shakespeare actually depicts them; and though there is much in the play that is foul-mouthed and calumnious, its overall configuration is demonstrably romantic and gracious. Clearly, an interpretation of the play which could unite these apparent contradictions would have the merit of arguing from rather than against the play's peculiar composition and would offer a possibility of granting it the kind of success which it can, in fact, achieve on stage. Just such an interpretation results if the play is understood as a species of tragicomedy.

The first step is to recognize that the various disjunctions in the play are deliberate and part of a pervasive and self-consciously paradoxical conception that is quite unlike that of Shakespeare's source. The very nature of love in the play, as Shaw saw, is paradoxical. The sexual roles are almost completely inverted: the woman pursues the man, chastity becomes the aggressor, the gentle female assumes the offensive. *All's Well* is a *Taming of the Shrew* in reverse, and from the perception of this fundamental paradox the play proliferates a host of others. Helena is at once sexually aggressive and chaste, Bertram at once passive and masculine. Her actions are instances both of her own will and of a will outside of her, while his have a value and effect quite contrary to what he supposes. Unlike his mentor Parolles, whose word of honor never becomes the deed, Bertram's deed of dishonor eventually becomes the word and act of honor.

Not only the action of the play, moreover, but its language and imagery are suffused with paradox. In the very first scene, in a dialogue that has distressed so many of the play's critics, Helena and Parolles debate the topic of virginity, Helena attempting to discover, at more than one level, "how virgins might blow up men," while Parolles descants bawdily upon variations of how "Virgins being blown down, man will quicklier be blown up" (I.i.119–20, 121–22). The debate, itself paradoxical, is a precise reflection and forecast of Helena's paradoxical predicament and it ends with a speech by Helena which is composed totally of paradoxes. She describes to Parolles the love which Bertram shall have:

> There shall your master have a thousand loves,
> A mother, and a mistress, and a friend,
> A phoenix, captain, and an enemy,
> A guide, a goddess, and a sovereign,
> A counselor, a traitress, and a dear;
> His humble ambition, proud humility,
> His jarring—concord, and his discord—dulcet;
> His faith, his sweet disaster; with a world

> Of pretty, fond, adoptious christendoms
> That blinking Cupid gossips.[7]
>   (I.i.162–71)

Not long afterwards, she talks to the Countess of her love for Bertram in similar terms, pleading that if the Countess

> Did ever, in so true a flame of liking,
> Wish chastely and love dearly, that your Dian
> Was both herself and love—O then, give pity
> To her whose state is such that cannot choose
> But lend and give where she is sure to lose;
> That seeks not to find that her search implies,
> But riddle-like lives sweetly where she dies!
>   (I.iii.206–12)

Similar riddles abound in the play. In arguing that the King should trust to her cure, Helena tells him that

> Great floods have flown
> From simple sources, and great seas have dried
> When miracles have by the great'st been denied.
> Oft expectation fails, and most oft there
> Where most it promises, and oft it hits
> Where hope is coldest and despair most sits.
>   (II.i.138–43)

Bertram writes to Helena that until he has "*no wife*" he has "*nothing in France*," and upon the report of her death, two lords use similar paradoxes to describe the inversion of Bertram's values:

Second Lord. I am heartily sorry that he'll be glad of this.
First Lord.   How mightily sometimes we make us comforts of our
                 losses!
Second Lord. And how mightily some other times we drown our
                 gain in tears! The great dignity that his valor hath here
                 acquir'd for him shall at home be encount'red with a shame
                 as ample.
>   (IV.iii.61–67)

Helena contrives a plot with the widow,

---

[7] This speech is puzzling and has been interpreted both as a satire upon courtly cults of love and as Helena's expression of her own love. The latter seems to me much more likely, but in any event the speech's paradoxical texture certainly reflects Helena's position as well as her own self-conscious feelings.

> which, if it speed,
> Is wicked meaning in a lawful deed,
> And lawful meaning in a lawful act,
> Where both not sin, and yet a sinful fact.
>   (III.vii.44–47)

Bertram boasts to Diana that "A heaven on earth I have won by wooing thee," and she replies, after his exit, "For which live long to thank both Heaven and me! / You may so in the end. . . . in this disguise, I think't no sin / To cozen him that would unjustly win" (IV.ii.66, 67–68, 75–76). As the play draws to a close, Helena twice assures the Widow (and us) that " 'the time will bring on summer'— / When briars shall have leaves as well as thorns / And be as sweet as sharp. . . . All's well that ends well" (IV.iv.31–33; V.i.25); and that end is itself revealed in a cascade of riddling paradoxes. When the King asks Diana why she has apparently wrongfully accused Bertram, she answers:

> Because he's guilty and he is not guilty.
> He knows I am no maid, and he'll swear to't;
> I'll swear I am a maid and he knows not.
>
> .   .   .   .   .
>   for this lord
> Who hath abus'd me as he knows himself—
> Though yet he never harm'd me—here I quit him.
> He knows himself my bed he hath defil'd;
> And at that time he got his wife with child.
> Dead though she be she feels her young one kick.
> So there's my riddle: one that's dead is quick,
> And now behold the meaning.
>   [*Re*]*enter* Widow [*with*] Helena
>   (V.iii.283–85, 291–98)

The preoccupation with riddles, oxymorons, and paradoxical oppositions is, of course, conventional in tragicomedy and an outgrowth of its basic pattern. According to the theory and practice of both Guarini and Fletcher the theatricality of a tragicomedy is a function of its capacity to accentuate and juxtapose the bitter and the sweet, and understood on this basis alone *All's Well* is more intelligible than many critics have found it. However, at the same time that Shakespeare unquestionably exploits this theatrical capital, he is also interested in exploring its deeper implications and possibilities, and at this level his debt to the tragicomic theater becomes even more significant and the play itself more interesting.

To begin with, the basic pattern of tragicomedy, as both Guarini and

Fletcher defined it—and as it was in fact practiced by coterie dramatists like Marston, even in ostensible comedies—placed primary stress not simply upon a mixture of comedy and tragedy but upon an action which came to a comic resolution despite or even because of its tragic possibilities; as Fletcher wrote, "A tragie-comedie is not so called in respect of mirth and killing, but in respect it wants deaths, which is inough to make it no tragedie, yet brings some neere it, which is inough to make it no comedie." For Fletcher this pattern was indeed to become an end in itself, a means of creating and sustaining peripeties of action and mood, but for Guarini, as we have seen, (and to a limited extent, Marston) the pattern became a theatrical expression of the paradox of the fortunate fall—and it is this paradox, with its unique reverberations, that unites and illuminates all the others in *All's Well*.

Whether Shakespeare was following Guarini's example directly in exploring the idea of *felix culpa* in tragicomedy or whether, independently, he discovered it to be implicit within the conventions of the form, it affects *All's Well* profoundly. The King refers to it directly in the closing lines of the play:

> All yet seems well, and if it end so meet,
> The bitter past, more welcome is the sweet;
> (V.iii.327–28)

but it is also inherent in the action. An ultimately beneficent Providence is a central protagonist of the play, and Helena throughout is explicitly associated with it, acting as its instrument and agent. She tells the Countess that the receipt from her father by which she hopes to cure the King "Shall for my legacy be sanctified / By th' luckiest stars in heaven," (I.iii.240–41) and when she persuades the King that "great floods have flown / From simple sources," her root paradox is that

> He that of greatest works is finisher
> Oft does them by the weakest minister.
> (II.i.135–36)

The King's cure is itself described as "*A showing of a heavenly effect in an earthly actor*," (II.iii.23–24) and from that time forward Helena bears the insignia of a Power that can transform sickness into health and sorrow into joy. After the Countess learns that Bertram has deserted her, she exclaims:

> What angel shall
> Bless this unworthy husband? He cannot thrive,
> Unless her prayers, whom heaven delights to hear

And loves to grant, reprieve him from the wrath
Of greatest justice.

(III.iv.25–29)

Helena herself assures the Widow that she should

> Doubt not but heaven
> Hath brought me up to be your daughter's dower,
> As it hath fated her to be my motive
> And helper to a husband.

(IV.iv.18–21)

Throughout *All's Well*, therefore, our responses to Helena and to the action which she generates are controlled by our awareness of the providential force which is working through them, and this awareness allows us at once to submit to the multiple paradoxes of the play and to stand above them, perceiving the pattern which they compose. As we have seen, tragicomedy conventionally demands such a "middle mood"[8] in order to assure us that the outcome will be comic and to enable us to appreciate its artifice. In *All's Well*, Shakespeare, like Guarini before him, was stimulated to relate this formal requirement to an understanding of experience itself.

In Shakespeare, as we would expect, this understanding is developed in ways and to a degree that are only suggested in *The Pastor Fido* and its successors, though the initial dramatic premises remain the same. To begin with, Shakespeare saw the extent to which the tragicomic dramatist could convert the audience's consciousness of the artifice of the playwright into an awareness of the artifice of Providence and thereby associate the workings of Providence with the dynamics of the play itself. This is a development which finds its fullest and most obvious expression in plays like *Measure for Measure* and *The Tempest*, where the Duke and Prospero act simultaneously "like power divine" and like theatrical producers, but it is evident in *All's Well* too. Helena directs a script for which she is at least in part responsible, and the last act especially is designed to make us conscious of the congruence of her theatrical and heavenly powers. Understood in this way, its obvious contrivance is a natural extension of the action of the play rather than a falsification or evasion of it. The very acuteness of the paradoxes which surround Helena, as well as her constant association with a force larger than herself, have compelled us from the start to remain at some distance from the action, and the last scene simply turns this sense of dis-

---

[8] The phrase is Una Ellis-Fermor's, *The Jacobean Drama* (London, 1936), p. 205.

engagement upon the play itself, enabling us to experience, rather than merely deduce, a union between the dispensations of the stage and of life.

This union, of course, is not simple. Helena in herself is neither an Olympian playwright nor Providence, whatever reverberations of both she may generate in the play, and though she may ultimately feel assured that all will end well, that assurance insulates neither her nor us from the experience of suffering. She can work a two-day miracle upon the King, but her redemption of the man she loves takes time and pain. Even her providential assurances are complicated and qualified. At the very moment that she tells the Widow that heaven has insured that she shall be Diana's dower, her thoughts turn to the actual experience of the bed trick, and she cannot help meditating upon the "strange men, / That can such sweet use make of what they hate." Moreover, though she may eventually reclaim Bertram from this strangeness, there are some men, notably Parolles, upon whom her miracles do not work at all.

Parolles, indeed, is a crucial instance, because by everyone's admission, including his own, he is irredeemable, and in any performance of the play his presence is as evident as Helena's and very nearly as important. His most apparent function is to personify the vice of dishonor which is within Bertram and at the same time to represent the kind of person whom Bertram, governed by such a vice, would find admirable. In this role he helps absorb some of the antagonism we feel toward Bertram, since as most recent productions have stressed, Bertram is young and naturally susceptible to Parolles's inducements. In this role he helps prepare us both directly and indirectly for Bertram's exposure and reclamation in the final scene, since the scene in which he is himself exposed is a moral cathartic for Bertram (who watches it) as well as an analogy, though a partial one, of Bertram's own fate at the hands of Helena.

In all these respects Parolles is easily intelligible and conventional, a humorous version of the standard tragicomic "villain." But he also has another dimension which is less usual. Like Helena, he has an expressive life of his own in the play, and one which is very nearly a contradiction of hers, for where she represents, both in herself and in her actions, what is gracious and redeemable in human relations, Parolles demonstrates what is postlapsarian and intractable. The scenes in which he is exposed, as many spectators have testified,[9] are powerful, and especially so because what is revealed is so familiar to him. Like the medieval Vice to whom he is related, the truth about himself does not make him free. When he is first unmasked one of the lords remarks, "Is

---

[9] See, e.g., Richard David, "Plays Pleasant and Plays Unpleasant," *Shakespeare Survey 8* (Cambridge, 1955), pp. 134–35.

it possible he should know what he is, and be that he is?" (IV.i.44–45) and the answer which he proceeds to enact in the scene is a profound yes. After he has been repudiated by Bertram and left in disgrace by the soldiers, he—again like his medieval forbears—explicitly and homiletically defends his identity for what it is, no more, no less:

> If my heart were great
> 'Twould burst at this. Captain I'll be no more,
> But I will eat and drink and sleep as soft
> As captain shall. Simply the thing I am
> Shall make me live. Who knows himself a braggart,
> Let him fear this; for it will come to pass
> That every braggart shall be found an ass.
> Rust, sword; cool, blushes; and Parolles live
> Safest in shame; being fool'd, by fool'ry thrive.
> There's place and means for every man alive.
> (IV.iii.319–28)

Earlier in the scene, while marveling at Bertram's betrayal of his wife and his apparent debauchery of Diana, a lord remarks, "As we are ourselves, what things we are!" (ll. 18–19). Parolles is a representation of the thing itself, at once a personification of the lowest common denominator of human nature and an enactment of it. Like Bertram, whose vicious tendencies he symbolizes, he is eventually accommodated in the gracious scheme of the play; Lafew, the one person besides Helena herself who knew him best, takes pity on him: "Sirrah, inquire further after me. . . . though you are a fool and a knave you shall eat" (V.ii.48–50). But no more than it is with Helena is this accommodation easy or pat. From the first, one of the constant ingredients of tragicomedy was satire, especially of court manners, and in the coterie drama of the early years of the seventeenth century, as we have seen, this element was dominant. Lavatch expresses some of the satiric impulses in more usual form, but in Parolles, Shakespeare, with his customary capacity to dilate conventional material, gives an expression to these impulses which reaches beyond manners and beyond satire itself. Parolles stands in *All's Well* as a perpetual point of reference, an embodiment of the irreducible human material which informs and qualifies all miracles.

There is one further ramification of tragicomedy in *All's Well* which is important to appreciate, and that is what Lafew calls "the rarest argument of wonder" (II.iii.7). Lafew applies the argument specifically to Helena's miraculous cure of the King, but wonder is a constituent of our response to much else in the play as well: our perception of the operation of *felix culpa* in the whole of the action, our simultaneous awareness of the ultimate graciousness of that paradox and of the indissoluble identities of its components, our sense of the congruence of Providence and art. Wonder indeed is the primary effect of *All's Well* and perhaps the most remarkable of Shakespeare's metamorphoses of contemporary tragicomic practice. Guarini had laid explicit stress upon the concomitant wonder of Providence and art, Marston turned the response toward a development of satiric detachment, and in Beaumont and Fletcher the sense of wonder was to be exploited to italicize theatricality. The Shakespearian wonder is all of these and more, for Shakespeare alone grasped the essential tragicomic principle which subsumed them. By definition, the action of tragicomedy constantly joins tragic and comic possibilities in a manner which encourages a conflation of emotions resulting in wonder. In *All's Well* this conflation is itself the very fabric of the drama, the subject of the action as well as its motive force, and as a consequence we experience wonder as an expression both of the form of the play and of the life which that form represents.

This sense of wonder is especially important in our reaction to Bertram, the character who so many critics insist destroys the play. Bertram stands somewhere between Helena and Parolles, morally as well as literally, illustrating potentialities of each. He is very young: as any production makes clear, only a boy. He is capable of real exploits of honor on the battlefield and of dishonor in the bedchamber. Like a boy, he can be cruel as well as lustful, and he is both, but he is not nearly as disturbing, for example, as Angelo in *Measure for Measure*, who is more mature and whose cruelty and lust are at once self-conscious and hypocritical. Bertram grossly abuses his heavenly wife and undervalues her, and that is a central paradox in a play which we have seen is filled with paradox, but he is neither evil nor, like Parolles, essentially irredeemable. He is, on the contrary, like the prodigal son of the parable (as well as of a number of prodigal plays written at this time),[10] whose reclamation is less a function of psychological or retributive logic than of the marvelous beneficence of Helena's love and of the Providence with which that love is associated; and at the end of the play Shakespeare does not show us a process of change in Bertram not because he cannot or because he refuses to compromise a portrait of nastiness,[11] but because he is most interested in stressing the highly paradoxical nature of the event itself. It is precisely when Bertram cannot conceivably sink any lower that he is delivered into his wife's redeeming arms—and then by a *coup de théâtre* that is as consciously contrived as it is gracious. The play-

[10] See Robert Y. Turner, "Dramatic Conventions in *All's Well That Ends Well*," *PMLA*, LXXV (1960), 497–502.

[11] A view held by Philip Edwards, *Shakespeare and the Confines of Art* (London, 1968), pp. 113–15. See also Muriel Bradbrook, *Shakespeare and Elizabethan Poetry* (London, 1951), pp. 162–70.

wright and Providence almost wittily join hands, and our response should be—what in fact it is in the theater—a feeling of admiration and wonder, the feelings exactly appropriate to tragicomedy.

A few critics, notably G. Wilson Knight and G. K. Hunter, have noticed that in this respect, as in others, including its concern with life's regenerative capacities, *All's Well* resembles the last plays.[12] Knight actually dates it around the time when *Pericles* and *The Winter's Tale* were composed and argues that like them it is a profoundly successful dramatization of transcendence and miracle. Hunter dates the play earlier, about 1604, and concludes that though it is most intelligible as an anticipation of the last plays, it had not yet mastered their idiom and is therefore, in the last analysis, straining for effects that it is not capable of assimilating.

I think that both critics are correct in drawing attention to the demonstrable analogies between *All's Well* and the last plays, but that in arguing for these analogies, each in a different way deprives it of its own integrity, Knight because he ultimately reduces the play to these analogies, and Hunter, curiously, because he eventually uses them against it. It is more just, and more fruitful, to look behind the analogies to their common source, which, as I have been suggesting, is tragicomedy, and to treat the plays not as a teleological development, but as distinct modulations of the same form.

There is no doubt a harmony and music in the final plays, particularly in their scenes of reunion and rebirth, which *All's Well* does not have, but it has a rhythm, not necessarily less valuable, which intersects the tragicomic curve at a different point and which can be equally successful on stage. It is hopeless to generalize about these plays, but it does seem clear that the centers of gravity of *Pericles, Cymbeline, The Winter's Tale, and The Tempest* are in the epiphanies of their endings and that the plays are in a sense written retrospectively. They not only draw towards the marvelous scenes with which they conclude but are throughout illuminated by the vision which these scenes create. This is true, as we shall see, even of *Cymbeline. All's Well*, on the other hand, like *Measure for Measure*, is concerned with an earlier stage of the tragicomic pattern and with the particularity of its elements. The terms of its paradoxes are thus deliberately, and even wittily, heightened, and its sense of strain becomes a part of its purpose. The treatment of Bertram is major evidence of this, but the difference is perhaps most easily discernible in the contrast between Parolles and a figure like Autolycas in *The Winter's Tale*. Autolycas is a knave, but sea-changed, directly

---

[12] Hunter, introduction to Arden edition, pp. liv–lvi; Knight, *The Sovereign Flower* (London, 1958), pp. 100–102 especially.

responsible for the play's concluding revelations, in himself almost a keynote of its final harmonies. Parolles, on the other hand, is incapable of song, and although he plays a role and has a place within the resolution of *All's Well*, he also stands outside of it, as uncompromisingly as Helena the thing he is. This does not lead to the kind of harmony which characterizes the last plays, but it rests upon an equally valid interpretation of the tragicomic spectrum, and it should not be denied either its integrity or its power.

Toward the end of *All's Well*, one of the lords remarks, "The web of our life is of a mingled yarn, good and ill together; our virtues would be proud if our faults whipp'd them not, and our crimes would despair if they were not cherish'd by our virtues" (IV.iii.68–71). The peculiar distinction of *All's Well* is that it so clearly delineates this mingling at the same time that it depicts the web which the yarn forms. In any performance of the play Parolles and Helena really have equal weight. They share the play like figures in a diptych: we cannot see or understand one without seeing and understanding the other. Tragicomedy had always been defined as a mixture of good and evil, and Guarini had stressed that this mixture was not merely a combination but a solution in which evil becomes converted into good. It was Shakespeare's genius in *All's Well* to discover that sadness was not merely a prelude to joy, but the means by which joy was itself to be apprehended, that the conjunction of good and evil constituted the mode in which both should be perceived. Like the medieval mystery plays, *All's Well That Ends Well* at once celebrates the presence of grace in human life and makes us comprehend the need for it.

Cymbeline

Like *All's Well, Cymbeline* is a difficult play to interpret, and for many of the same reasons. It seems composed of discontinuities and discords which resist coherent analysis. The action, half-romance, half-history, moves freely through a kaleidoscope of milieux: a primitive British court, a Machiavellian Italy, a Roman Italy, a pastoral cave. The hero is at best only half-admirable: in the beginning he loves Imogen and values her as "the gift of the gods" (I.v.88); after Iachimo's deception he orders her death. Its principal villain is similarly only half-sinister: at possibly his most evil moment, when he is attempting to seduce Imogen, Iachimo becomes so intoxicated with his own verbal extravagance that he subverts his own intentions. Cloten, a lesser villain to begin with, is also a clownish boor, as Shakespeare takes pains to establish in the scene with the Second Lord (I.iii); the Queen is never more than a cardboard figure; and Cymbeline is not, until the end, much more than a dupe. Imogen, the principal and unifying figure of interest in the play, is less equivocally portrayed, since in herself she is consistent enough. But on the other hand, the play deals with her very strangely. In a scene that is studiously prepared for, she awakens by the headless body of Cloten, who is dressed in Posthumous's garments, and mistaking him for her husband, she sings "an aria of agony." It is a moving and convincing one, but we cannot help being conscious, at the same time, as Granville-Barker remarks, that "it is a fraud on Imogen; and we are accomplices in it."[13] No other heroine in Shakespeare, Helena included, suffers this kind of exploitation.

Faced with such apparent contradictions, most critics have taken refuge in allegory, or in apocalyptic sentimentalizations (of Imogen especially), or in disintegrations of the text. Yet, as with *All's Well*, a better answer would seem to be that the play is an attempt to explore the techniques and implications of tragicomic dramaturgy, and it is a better answer because it is based on the plausible assumption that Shakespeare is doing what he wants to do (more or less successfully, as the case may be) and that what appear to be contradictions in the play are deliberate and part of its very nature. Even superficially considered, most of the features of the play which cause trouble for critics are precisely those which are most typical of self-conscious tragicomedy. Posthumous, in his sudden turn of heart (and subsequent counterturn), is not unlike countless Fletcherian heroes whose discontinuous characterizations provide the occasions for turns of plot and emotional declamations; and when at the end of the play he strikes his disguised wife to the ground, the theatrical effect is not so very unlike that provided by Philaster's wounding of Arathusa or of the disguised Euphrasia. Fletcher's scenes are obviously not as resonant as Shakespeare's, but the theatrical situations and patterns are nevertheless initially the same. Similarly, Iachimo is very like the villains who abound in Marston's plays—so close to parodies, so consumed with their own flamboyant rhetoric, and so eventually powerless that though they arouse our apprehensions we cannot take them entirely seriously. Granville-Barker says of Iachimo that "he presents us, in his arrogance, with an approach to a travesty of himself, which is also a travesty of the very medium in which he exists. A subtle and daring piece of craftsmanship, germane to this hybrid tragi-comedy. Instead of opposing the heroic and the comic, Shakespeare blends the two."[14] There could be no better description of the kind of effect to be found in Marston's experiments in tragicomedy, and the notion in particular of Iachimo's "travesty of the very medium in which

[13] *Prefaces to Shakespeare*, I (Princeton, 1952), 539.
[14] Ibid., p. 502.

he exists" goes to the heart not only of Marston's method but of the method of much of the private theater.

Imogen, shaped in a more familiar Shakespearian mold, cannot be explained so easily. Like Helena, she has a depth and vitality which no character in Marston, and still less in Fletcher, can match. She has a "tune" of her own (V.v.239), and she is the only character in the play with whom we are really asked to sympathize. There is no emotional indirection or ambivalence, for example, about her reception of the news that Posthumous doubts her, nor is there any in our reaction to it:

> *Pis.* What shall I need to draw my sword? the paper
> Hath cut her throat already.
>
> .   .   .   .   .
>
> *Imo.* False to his bed? What is it to be false?
> To lie in watch there, and to think on him?
> To weep 'twixt clock and clock? If sleep charge Nature,
> To break it with a fearful dream of him,
> And cry myself awake? That's false to's bed, is it?
> (III.iv.32–33, 40–44)

But if Imogen in herself seems remote from the usual heroines of tragi-comedy, the situations in which she is placed are not. She is repeatedly called upon for histrionic displays in much the same way that Marston's heroines or Fletcher's are—through contrived misunderstandings, or mistaken identities, or deceptions. Her grief over the supposed dead body of her husband, moving certainly in itself, is not different in kind from the grief which Maria displays in *The Malcontent* when her disguised husband is apparently attempting to seduce her. Imogen is made to perform for us, and she is, throughout, exploited not only by plotters but—again like Helena—by the plot of the play itself. It is not surprising that there should be a slightly irascible lilt to her tune—Shakespeare's own unconscious reflex, perhaps, as well as hers, against the treatment to which she is subjected.

Not only the characters and the plot, moreover, are symptomatic of the play's self-conscious contrivance; everything about *Cymbeline* suggests that Shakespeare "is somehow *playing* with the play."[15] Its verse draws attention to itself: a "new Euphuism," Granville-Barker calls it, where often "the thought or emotion behind" a speech seems "too far-fetched for the occasion or the speaker"; and its stagecraft consistently requires a style of "sophisticated artlessness."[16] Granville-Barker's re-

---

[15] Frank Kermode, *Shakespeare: The Final Plays* (London, 1963), p. 22.
[16] *Prefaces*, I, 498, 466.

marks about the kind of performance the play demands are worth quoting at length:

He has an unlikely story to tell, and in its unlikelihood lies not only its charm, but largely its very being; reduce it to reason, you would wreck it altogether. Now in the theater there are two ways of dealing with the inexplicable. If the audience are to take it seriously, leave it unexplained. They will be anxious—pathetically anxious—to believe you; with faith in the dose, they will swallow a lot. The other plan is to show one's hand, saying in effect: 'Ladies and gentlemen, this is an exhibition of tricks, and what I want you to enjoy among other things is the skill with which I hope to perform them.' This art, which deliberately displays its art, is very suited to a tragicomedy, to to the telling of a serious story that must yet not be taken too seriously, lest its comedy be swamped by its tragedy and a happy ending become too incongruous.[17]

This could serve equally well as a prescription for performance of Guarini or Marston or Fletcher, and in this respect, as in others, it is evident that *Cymbeline*, like *All's Well*, can best be understood as a form of tragicomedy.

The ways in which Shakespeare exploited the capacities of this form in *Cymbeline* are, of course, remarkable, and distinct both from the practice of his contemporaries and of his own earlier problem plays. To begin with, *Cymbeline*, even more than *All's Well*, is governed by a pattern of action made intelligible by the paradox of the fortunate fall. The idea is unusually explicit in the play. Lucius tells the disguised Imogen:

> Be cheerful; wipe thine eyes:
> Some falls are means the happier to arise;
> (IV.ii.402–3)

and shortly afterwards, Jupiter, the play's presiding deity, informs Posthumous's parents in a dream that

> Whom best I love I cross; to make my gift,
>   The more delay'd, delighted. Be content,
> Your low-laid son our godhead will uplift:
>   His comforts thrive, his trials well are spent:
> Our Jovial star reign'd at his birth, and in
>   Our temple was he married. Rise, and fade.
> He shall be lord of lady Imogen,
>   And happier much by his affliction made.
> (V.iv.101–8)

---

[17] Ibid., pp. 466–67.

As in *All's Well*, a primary manifestation of the influence of this idea upon the action of the play is the concern with riddle and paradox. It is most obvious in the actual riddle which Posthumous finds in his cell, the explication of which concludes the play, but it is apparent elsewhere as well. The language of *Cymbeline* is saturated with paradoxes. The Queen, Imogen remarks, "can tickle where she wounds," and the King "buys" her "injuries, to be friends" (I.ii.16, 36). After giving the Queen a harmless sleeping potion, the doctor remarks that

> there is
> No danger in what show of death it makes,
> More than the locking up the spirits a time,
> To be more fresh, reviving. She is fool'd
> With a most false effect: and I the truer,
> So to be false with her.
>
>   (I.vi.39–44)

The Queen tells Cloten that in wooing Imogen he must "make denials / Increase" his "services" (II.iii.49–50), and Cloten instructs Pisanio to accept villainy as good:

Sirrah, if thou wouldst not be a villain, but do me true service, undergo those employments wherein I should have cause to use thee with a serious industry, that is, what villainy soe'er I bid thee do, to perform it, directly and truly, I would think thee an honest man.

                                                    (III.v.109–115)

Pisanio himself, who is cast in the role of Imogen's executioner and yet is the means of her preservation, speaks constantly in self-conscious paradoxes which mirror his predicament. After sending Cloten in pursuit of Imogen, he soliloquizes:

> Thou bid'st to my loss: for true to thee
> Were to prove false, which I will never be,
> To him that is most true. To Milford go,
> And find not her whom thou pursuest. Flow, flow,
> You heavenly blessings, on her! This fool's speed
> Be cross'd with slowness; labour be his meed!
>   (III.v.162–67)

Later, he complains that he remains

> Perplex'd in all. The heavens still must work.
> Wherein I am false, I am honest; not true, to be true.
> These present wars shall find I love my country,

Even to the note o' th' king, or I'll fall in them:
All other doubts, by time let them be clear'd
Fortune brings in some boats that are not steer'd.
(IV.iii.41–46)

Not long afterwards, Posthumous welcomes his imprisonment: "Most welcome bondage; for thou art a way, / I think to liberty" (V.iv.3–4). The Gaoler jests with him about his coming hanging, comparing him to a man paying a reckoning at a tavern:

sorry that you have paid too much, and sorry that you are paid too much: purse and brain, both empty: the brain the heavier for being too light; the purse too light, being drawn of heaviness. O, of this contradiction you shall now be quit. O, the charity of a penny cord!

(V.iv.163–69)

Posthumous's answer is, "I am merrier to die than thou art to live" (V.iv.174), but the play's charity is of another kind, though equally paradoxical. In the revelation of Imogen's life, Cymbeline feels that the gods mean to strike him "To death with mortal joy;" Posthumous, once more in Imogen's embrace, vows to "Hang there like fruit, my soul, / Till the tree die," and he forgives Iachimo, saying, "The power that I have on you, is to spare you: / The malice towards you, to forgive you" (V.v.235, 263, 419–20). There are "Some griefs," as Imogen remarks earlier, which "doth physic love" (III.ii.33–34).

There is another strain of paradox in *Cymbeline*, less obviously related to the idea of *felix culpa*, but perhaps even more significant. When Posthumous joins the British army in the habit of a peasant, he remarks that "To shame the guise o' th' world, I will begin, / The fashion less without, and more within" (V.i.32–33), and throughout the play there is a deep preoccupation with the frequently paradoxical oppositions between body and soul, between what human beings look like on the outside and what they are within, between their garments and their natures. Cymbeline is "O'ercome" with the Queen's "show" (V.v.54), and when he learns the full extent of her treachery from the doctor, he can only remark:

                    Mine eyes
Were not in fault, for she was beautiful:
Mine ears that heard her flattery, nor my heart
That thought her like her seeming. It had been vicious
To have mistrusted her.
                    (V.v.62–66)

Imogen enrages Cloten by telling him that he is not worthy of comparison with Posthumous's "mean'st garment" (II.iii.134), and in a grotesque effort to revenge the insult upon his "noble and natural person" (III.v.139–40), he literally dons that garment and plans to ravish her in it. Instead, he meets Guiderius, a true prince clothed as a peasant; challenges him to yield: "Thou villain base, / Know'st me not by my clothes?"; receives the answer, "No, nor thy tailor, rascal, / Who is thy grandfather: he made those clothes, / Which (as it seems) make thee" (IV.ii.80–83); and loses his head. Guiderius himself, as well as his brother Arviragus, both long lost sons of Cymbeline, are constantly presented as having natures which are belied by their appearance. Belarius, their abductor and guardian, tells Imogen not to "measure our good minds / By this rude place we live in" (III.vii.37–38), and on several other occasions, marvels at how "Nature" prompts the boys, "though trained up thus meanly ... In simple and low things to prince it, much / Beyond the trick of others" (III.iii.82–86), at how "an invisible instinct should frame them / To royalty unlearn'd, honour untaught, / Civility not seen from other...." (IV.ii.177–79), and at how "their blood thinks scorn / Till it fly out and show them princes born" (IV.iv.52–53). Posthumous, a commoner, is at the start of the play praised for his fair union of outer and inner manhood—"I do not think," says one of the gentlemen, "So fair an outward, and such stuff within / Endows a man, but he" (I.i.22–24)—but because of Iachimo's show, the balance is disrupted. Pisanio condemns the very paper in which Posthumous announces Imogen's alleged infidelity: "Senseless bauble, / Art thou a foedary for this act, and look'st / So virgin-like without," (III.ii.20–22); and Imogen herself, when she learns of his suspicions, laments that she has become "a garment out of fashion," and that "All good seeming," because of Posthumous's revolt, "shall be thought / Put on for villainy; not born where't grows, / But worn a bait for ladies." (III.iv.51, 54–57) Posthumous eventually reclaims himself, achieving both Imogen and his own wholeness, but only by inverting these disparities, assuming a penitential garment, "the fashion less without, and more within," and fighting as a "poor soldier ... so richly" that his "rags sham'd gilded arms." (V.v.3–4)

Imogen alone in the play is able from the start to bridge such disjunctions, both in herself and in her perception of others. In Iachimo's words, her virtue rests precisely in the identity of her nature and her appearance:

> All of her that is out of door most rich!
> If she be furnish'd with a mind so rare,
> She is alone th' Arabian bird.
>   (I.vii.15–17)

All the other characters are either incapable of such union or must learn to achieve it, and much of the action of the play is concerned with the process by which they literally assume and emerge from disguise. Even Imogen herself must wear a disguise, albeit as Fidele, and can only reveal herself when her other name has been cleared.

The insistence upon garments in this play is remarkable, even in comparison with the Shakespearian romantic comedies in which disguise is paramount. It partly represents a continuation of the concern expressed in *All's Well* with the relationship between virtue and breeding. Like Cloten, Parolles too is accused of having been made by his tailor (though he does not suffer as badly for it), and his very name signifies the play's interest in the discrepancies between word and deed, appearance and true nature. The extensive use of the theatrical symbolism of clothing in *Cymbeline* serves to explore these same ideas, as does the whole configuration of a plot in which both nobility and villainy are in disguise.

There is, however, a further significance to the preoccupation with dress in *Cymbeline* which marks a turn of the paradox of the fortunate fall that is peculiar to the last plays. It is an idea stated and dramatized most directly by *The Winter's Tale*: in the words of the shepherd who finds Perdita, "Thou met'st with things dying, I with things new-born" (III.iii.111–12). *Cymbeline* enacts this pattern more symbolically, primarily through the medium of disguise and the surrounding context of paradoxical inversions. Cloten, dressed as Posthumous, is consumed by a fantasy of raping Imogen, which is as much a travesty of the creation of life as his costume is of himself, and he finds a literal death. Imogen accepts the identity of Fidele as an act of despair, because, as she tells Pisanio, "How live? / Or in my life what comfort, when I am / Dead to my husband?" (III.iv.129–31); and in that disguise she appears to die in her brothers' cave, only to be "more fresh, reviving." Posthumous, to whom she also seems dead, himself takes on a habit of despair: "so I'll die / For thee, O Imogen, even for whom my life / Is every breath, a death" (V.i.25–27); and in that habit he helps redeem both himself and his country. In yet another disguise in prison—as a Roman— he talks of the liberty of bondage and of his merry wish for the charity of death, but he dreams of the different charity of Jupiter, finds a book which is "not, as is our fangled world, a garment / Nobler than that it covers" (V.iv.134–35), and reads the riddle that eventually explains the renewal of life of his family and his kingdom.

In the final recognition scene of the play, all these movements are gathered together and brought to fulfillment in what is explicitly recognized as an act of birth. The Queen's "show" is revealed, as is Iachimo's and Cloten's; Posthumous, Imogen, Guiderius, Arviragus, and Belarius emerge from their garments to assume their true identities, their ap-

pearances at peace now with their real natures; and Cymbeline, struck
"to death with mortal joy" at the revelation of his daughter and sons,
declares,

> O what am I?
> A mother to the birth of three? Ne'er mother
> Rejoic'd deliverance more. Blest pray you be,
> That, after this strange starting from your orbs,
> You may reign in them now. O Imogen,
> Thou hast lost by this a kingdom.

Imogen replies, "No, my lord; / I have got two worlds by't" (V.v.369–
75). In the death of the Queen and Cloten and in the rebirth of the
King's heirs, the kingdom of Britain too is reborn, literally delivered
from evil, its identity baptized in battle, its life within a vision of Pax
Romana confirmed.

The idea of death and rebirth is suggested more than once in *All's
Well*—"there's my riddle, one that's dead is quick"—but it operates primarily on a verbal level. In *Cymbeline*, as in the last plays in general, it
informs the action profoundly, becoming associated with the tragicomic
paradoxes both of nature and Christianity. Early in the play, before his
fall, Posthumous states that he is ready to "abide the change of time, /
Quake in the present winter's state, and wish / That warmer days
would come" (II.iv.4–6), and there are other references in the play
which similarly relate human history to the birth and death of the sea-
sons. This is a primary function of the pastoral scenes, especially of Imogen's death, when Arviragus strews flowers upon her, sings his famous
dirge, and her revival becomes visually as well as verbally associated
with the rejuvenating powers of the earth. At the same time there are, as
we have seen, various references, many of them explicit, to the central
Christian paradox of the fortunate fall, and the action itself, with its
multiple disguises, bears particular overtones of the casting off (and in
Cloten's case, the literal death) of the old Adam and the birth of the
new, both in individuals and in the kingdom. Posthumous's penitential transformation especially is strongly inscribed on the ending of the
play.[18]

But even more important than these particular adumbrations, which
are in any case more fully expressed in *Pericles, The Winter's Tale*, and

---

[18] Northrop Frye, *A Natural Perspective* (New York, 1965), pp. 66–67, argues
that the choice of Cymbeline's reign as the time of the play, the remarks of the
oracular jailer, and the numerous references to the peace of Augustus are all
meant to suggest the contemporaneous birth of Christ.

The Tempest, is the degree to which in *Cymbeline,* as in these other plays, the dynamics of tragicomedy become a means of expressing the human creative process and the genesis of the play becomes wholly and marvelously indistinguishable from the evolution of the providential pattern which it represents. As we have seen, this association is explored by Shakespeare in both *All's Well* and *Measure for Measure.* In neither of these earlier plays, however, not even in *All's Well,* which includes the miracle of the King's regeneration, is there the same emphasis as in the later plays upon the corresponding unity of the dramatist's creative powers and those of life itself. This unity is perhaps most perfect in *The Tempest,* where Prospero is both a playwright and a presiding deity and the theme of creative transformation is at once profound and explicit, but its essential outlines are present in *Cymbeline* as well. The scene, for example, where Imogen awakens beside the headless body of Cloten clothed as her husband is entirely symptomatic. It is indeed the "fraud" that Granville-Barker said it is, but deliberately not accidentally so, a fraud like the multiple disguises in the play, of which we are meant to be conscious; and when Imogen responds to the situation with rather precious classical imagery, her speech too is intended to be observed as much as felt. We are clearly intended to watch Shakespeare directing his characters, and more particularly, to observe how his own paradoxical capacity as a dramatist to transform illusion into reality corresponds to a human capacity for regeneration and transformation. It is therefore profoundly appropriate that in the last scene, in which the show of evil is finally exposed, in which all of the paradoxes of the play meet and are resolved, and in which most of the principal characters are delivered from literal disguise to be figuratively reborn, that in this scene Posthumous should strike the disguised Imogen to the ground and say to her, "Shall's have a play of this? Thou scornful page, / There lie thy part" (V.v.228–29). It is a line which italicizes the full wonder of the moment, both because our own rejoicing is a function of our experience of the labor and births of the playwright as well as of the characters, and because Posthumous's action itself dramatizes that mysterious union of joy and pain which is akin to childbirth and which at its deepest reach is the true miracle of the last plays.

The effect of this union is most fully analyzed in the first gentleman's account of the reunion of Perdita and her father in *The Winter's Tale:*

the changes I perceived in the king and Camillo were very notes of admiration: they seemed almost, with staring on one another, to tear the cases of their eyes: there was speech in their dumbness, language in their very gesture; they looked as they had heard of a world ransomed, or one destroyed: a notable passion of wonder appeared in them; but the wisest be-

holder, that knew no more but seeing, could not say if th' importance were
joy or sorrow; but in the extremity of the one it must needs be.

(V.ii.10–19)

The sense of epiphany which this describes is most acute in the scenes of
reunion which are at once the culminations and the well-springs of the
last plays—the reunion of Pericles with Marina, Cymbeline with Imogen, Leontes himself with both Hermione and Perdita, and the court
party with Ferdinand and Miranda—but the conjunction of extremities
which characterizes these scenes is not confined to them alone. Caliban
and Ariel, Marina in a brothel, the whole diptych construction of
The Winter's Tale, Imogen pursued by Cloten and vilified by her husband—all are manifestations of the same kind of experience. It is a
phenomenon which can be seen from a number of perspectives, not least
the mystery of Christ, but it can also be regarded as Shakespeare's supreme formal transmutation of the characteristic antitheses of tragicomedy.[19] As in *All's Well*, the terms of these antitheses are distinct and
indissoluble, but the extremity with which they are represented and opposed dilates them until they truly do seem to meet in a new birth which
strikes us, no less than Cymbeline, "with mortal joy."

[19] Romance, of course, characteristically develops and conflates such antitheses,
and Shakespeare was certainly also responding to that genre in his last plays. See
Stanley Wells, "Shakespeare and Romance," in *Later Shakespeare*, eds. Brown
and Harris (New York, 1967), pp. 48–79. The advantage, if not necessity, of stressing tragicomedy is that it offers specifically dramatic analogues and is therefore
capable of illuminating Shakespeare's actual theatrical practice. For further discussion of this point, see Arthur C. Kirsch, "*Cymbeline* and Coterie Dramaturgy,"
ELH, XXXIV (1967), 285–306; and Bernard Harris, " 'What's past is prologue':
Cymbeline and *Henry VIII*," in *Later Shakespeare*, pp. 203–229. Cf. Norman Rabkin, *Shakespeare and the Common Understanding* (New York, 1967), pp. 205–12,
for the view that *Cymbeline* fails to unite its formal self-consciousness with its thematic concerns.

V

Middleton

CONTRARY to T. S. Eliot's rather remarkable assertion that Middleton is "merely the name which associates six or seven great plays," that he had no "point of view" or "message,"[1] the impress of Middleton's artistic personality upon his works is actually extraordinary. He wrote many different kinds of dramatic works under a variety of circumstances, but all of them, coterie as well as public theater plays, comedies as well as tragicomedies and tragedies, those written with collaborators as well as those he wrote alone, and those which are not great as well as those which are—all reveal an identical and powerful dramatic "point of view." It has its roots, I think, in Middleton's apprenticeship in the private theater, and behind that, in the morality play, but it is in any case immediately recognizable in all his plays, as the following quotations from three of them show. The plays are of different genres and are widely separated in time, spanning the whole course of his career. The first is *Michaelmas Term*, a comedy performed in about 1606 by the Children of Pauls. Shortly after completing his gulling of Easy, Quomodo decides to feign death in order to observe how his family will act, "because," as he says in a soliloquy,

I see before mine eies that most of our heires prove notorious Rioters after our deaths, and that cousonage in the father wheeles about to follie in the sonne, our posteritie commonly foylde at the same weapon, at which we plaide rarely. And being the worlds beaten worde, what's got over the Divels backe, (that's by knaverie) must be spent under his bellie, (that's by lechery): being awake in these knowings, why should not I oppose 'em now, and breake destinie of her custome, preventing that by pollicie, which without it must needes be Destinie?[2]

(IV.i.86–96)

---

[1] *Selected Essays* (London, 1934), p. 162.
[2] References to the texts of the following plays are to the first editions: *The Family of Love* (London, 1608); *A Trick to Catch the Old One* (London, 1608); *Your Five Gallants* (London, ca. 1608); *A Mad World, My Masters* (London, 1608); *Michaelmas Term* (London, 1607); *A Chaste Maid in Cheapside* (London, 1630); *More Dissemblers Besides Women* (London, 1657); *A Fair Quarrel* (London, 1617); *The Old Law* (London, 1656); *Women Beware Women* (London, 1657); and *The Changeling* (London, 1653). Act, scene, and line references to

About ten years later, in a soliloquy in the tragicomedy *More Dissem-blers Besides Women*, Aurelia, who is using Andrugio's courtship of her to reach her lover Lactantio, states:

> I smile
> To think how I have fitted him with an office;
> His love takes pains to bring our loves together,
> Much like your man that labors to get treasure,
> To keep his wife high for anothers pleasure.
> (II.iii.104–8)

Finally, in the tragedy *Women Beware Women*, performed in about 1625, Leantio exclaims in an aside as he watches the Duke steal his wife, his "life's best treasure," away from him (as he himself had stolen her away from her family):

> So, so;
> Here stands the poor theif now that stole the treasure,
> And he's not thought on, ours is near kin now
> To a twin-misery born into the world.
> First comes the hard conscienc'd-worlding, he hoords wealth up,
> Then comes the next, and he feasts all upon't;
> One's damn'd for getting, th'other for spending on't:
> O equal Justice, thou has't met my sin
> With a full weight, I'm rightly now opprest,
> All her friends heavy hearts lie in my Brest.
> (III.ii.87–96)

There are many revealing parallels among these speeches, but the most important are that their means of perception are the same and that their ironies lead to similar kinds of theatrical response. Quomodo's pairing of cozenage and folly, knavery and lust, is metaphorically as well as substantively comparable to Aurelia's conjunction of avarice and lechery and to Leantio's twin-misery, hoarding and feasting, getting and spending; and all the images are ironically enacted in comparable ways. Quomodo, who has cozened for gain of land and money, is shortly cuckolded by his wife and made destitute by the folly of his son; Aurelia is in the end abandoned by Lactantio for the Duchess, who has in fact been using him as Aurelia had been using Andrugio; and Leantio, whose theft of Bianca, as his own words make clear, is craft for gain

---

these plays are to *The Works of Thomas Middleton*, ed. A. H. Bullen, 8 vols. (London, 1885–86). References to *Hengist* are to the edition of R. C. Bald (New York, 1938), and references to *The Witch* are to the Malone Society edition of W. W. Greg and F. P. Wilson (Oxford, 1950).

of "treasure," has been made bankrupt in love, if not in money, by the lust and folly of his wife and mother. Moreover, in the deepest sense, all three characters are foiled by the same weapon with which they played: the knave Quomodo by the very policy with which he hopes to defeat destiny; the duplicitous Aurelia by the dissembling which infects her whole society; and the factor Leantio, more subtly, by an intrinsically mercenary nature which can cherish love only as a commodity and is therefore inevitably outbid for it. The closeness of these correspondences is not accidental, for the same dramatic intelligence is at work in each of these speeches and is occupied with the same kinds of themes and effects.

The similarity of these themes and effects is evident in all the plays.[3] The irony of sin's inevitable self-retribution, in particular, is a keynote of both the language and action of every genre Middleton explored, and as in Jonson, the idea is not in any way an anticipation of Rymer's notion of poetical justice, but rather a whole conception of the conditions of human behavior, a moral psychology. What is finally most fascinating about Quomodo, for example, is, as the judge tells him at the end of the play: "Thou art thine owne affliction" (V.iii.170). This is the truth that Middleton dramatizes most deeply, both with his comic gulls and his less comic sinners.

The themes of self-deceit as well as self-defeat saturate the city comedies. The plot of *Your Five Gallants* consists of a perfect circle of gullings, a seventeenth-century *La Ronde* of usury and lust:

does my boy pick, & I steale, to enrich my selfe, to keepe her, to maintaine him: why this is right the sequence of the world, A L. maintaines her, she maintaines a Knight, he maintaines a Whore, shee maintaines a captaine. So, in like manner, the pocket keepes my boye, hee keepes me, I keepe her, shee keepes him; it runs like quick-silver from one to another.

                                                                 (III.ii.100–107)

In one of the central scenes of *The Family of Love*, Lipsalve and Gudgeon, because of their desires to enjoy Glister's wife, are gulled by him into literally scourging one another, and as we watch them Glister comments: "men can not find / Lust ever better handled in his kind" (III.vi. 34–35). The self-betrayal of folly dominates the whole of *A Mad World, My Masters*. "For craft recoyles in the end, like an overcharg'd musket,"

---

[3] For discussions of the integrity of Middleton's work see Richard H. Barker, *Thomas Middleton* (New York, 1958), and a work published too late to be assimilated in this study, David M. Holmes, *The Art of Thomas Middleton* (Oxford, 1971). See also Richard Levin, *The Multiple Plot in English Renaissance Drama* (Chicago, 1971) for an analysis of Middleton's use of double plots.

says Follywit, "and maymes the very hand that puts fire too't" (III.iii.
11–13); and much of the pleasure of the play consists both in observing
Follywit put this principle into practice by capitalizing upon his uncle's
"bounteousness," and in seeing him fall victim to it himself as he marries his uncle's whore. "Who lives by cunning," as his uncle points out
in the last lines of the play, "marke it, his fates cast, / When he has guld
all, then is himselfe the last" (V.ii.298–99). The same pattern is evident
in *A Trick to Catch the Old One*, where the delight of Witgood's intrigue is that he gulls the rivals Lucre and Hoard by making them
believe that they are gulling each other. As Hoard himself says, again
in the last line of the play, "Who seeme most crafty prove oft times most
fooles" (V.ii.207). In *Michaelmas Term* itself the principle is equally
obvious. Quomodo, like Follywit, describes the irony of the self-defeat
of craft and is himself subject to it. He has taught his wife Thomasine
and Easy precisely the craft which they use to dispossess him, he pre-
dicts knavery yielding to the lechery of his wife and cozenage yielding
to the folly of his son, and—most ironic of all—he brings both about by
his own "knowing" intrigue to prevent them. In *A Chaste Maid in
Cheapside*, finally, there is a similar though more complex network of
ironies. "Some onely can get riches and no Children," like the Kixes,
others "onely can get Children and no riches," like the Touchwood
Seniors (II.i.11–12); thinking to gull an innocent country girl, the
avaricious promoters are left with her bastard; the jeweler Yellowham-
mer's greed blinds him into unknowingly fitting a wedding ring for
his own daughter; Sir Walter Whorehound plays upon his capital value
in order to satisfy his lust and is ultimately rejected when that value
is depleted. Lust and avarice ceaselessly spawn and consume each other
in the play, and eventually no character is exempt from the remorseless
continuum which they form.

Middleton's tragicomedies are concerned with a similar continuum.
All the deceitful protagonists of *More Dissemblers Besides Women* are
themselves deceived by precisely the impulses they play upon: the Duchess and Aurelia by sexual desire, Lactantio and the Cardinal by greed
and ambition. In a plot comparable to that of *Your Five Gallants*, the
conventional cross-purposes of comedy (Aurelia uses Andrugio to court
Lactantio; the Duchess uses Lactantio to court Andrugio; both women
have contempt for the man whom they use; both are scorned by the
man they really want) are translated into an emblem of the self-
sustaining economy of folly and sin. Though less symmetrically, Middleton's three other major tragicomedies dramatize similar patterns of
behavior and thought. In *The Witch* the supernatural influence of
potions and magic ribbons comes eventually to symbolize (however

imperfectly) the principle that "each mans punishment proves still a kind of Justice to himself" (V.i.58–59); and in both *The Old Law* and *The Fair Quarrel* the characters who consciously deceive or abuse others are all ultimately made victims of their own deceptions.

The same irony is present in the tragedies and exerts particularly profound effects upon characterization. The simplest of the group, *Hengist*, is melodramatically full of self-gullings. The early part of the play is consumed with Vortiger's schemes to vex the King from the throne, all of which ironically rebound upon himself. As the play develops, Vortiger, who is now King, becomes the dupe of Hersus, who convinces him to repudiate his wife and marry the pagan Roxena, who is in reality Hersus's whore. In the climactic scene of the play Vortiger and Hersus are alone on the castle walls. Vortiger is faced with a revolt because of his marriage to Roxena and tries to place the blame for the marriage upon Hersus. Hersus answers: "twas the Councell / Of your owne Lust & blood; your appetite knows it" (V.ii.74–75). Vortiger then stabs Hersus in an attempt to quiet him and placate the crowd below, and Hersus in turn reveals to him that he has been gulled all along, that Roxena is a whore. Wild with rage, both men stab each other with words and knives, as a spectator comments:

> See sin needes
> Noe more distruction then it breedes
> In it[s] owne Bosome.
>   (V.ii.107–9)

In *Women Beware Women*, Leantio meets an equal justice in much the same way. His long soliloquies in the opening scenes of the play establish that Bianca is inseparable from goods in his mind and that both are fundamentally objects of lust. His speeches are permeated by images of the world of commodity and purchasing and selling, and in this world his best "treasure" is Bianca and his best "business" is to make love to her. So he loses her, as we have seen, partly, as he himself takes pains to explain, because the Duke is only stealing what he himself stole, but more significantly and far more ironically than even he understands, because of the necessary self-defeat of the mercenary lust by which his love is defined. In a world of lustful commodity, the Duke is inevitably the better businessman, Bianca inevitably vulnerable to the sexual prowess of superior wealth and power. Leantio is himself bought, not only by the Duke. who pays him with a captainship to submit to cuckoldom quietly, but by Livia, who literally buys his manhood with clothes and footmen and race horses:

Liv. Do but you love enough, I'll give enough.
Lean. Troth then, I'll love enough, and take enough.
Liv. Then we are both pleas'd enough.

(III.ii.375–77)

It is only the last of a long series of ironies in Leantio's career that he should finally be eliminated because he is driven to boast to Bianca of the high price his sale has fetched. The portrait of Leantio is completely dispassionate in its penetration of the self-defeat of his insensitivity and lust, yet also poignant in its subtle comprehension of the degree to which his nature is necessarily an instance, a reflection, of the moral condition of the whole world of the play. The orgy at the end of the play in which all the gulled gullers destroy themselves is merely a blatant extension of this conception.

In *The Changeling*, the most striking instance of the irony of self-deception, of course, is Beatrice Joanna. She uses Deflores and is ultimately used by him, embracing the "basilisk" she has shunned, and gradually loving what she has loathed: "The East is not more beauteous then his service" (V.i.71); and she does so because she must, because from the start she wore Deflores in her own bosom:

> Beneath the starres, upon yon Meteor
> Ever h[u]ng my fate, 'mongst things corruptible,
> I ne're could pluck it from him, my loathing
> Was Prophet to the rest, but ne're beleev'd
> Mine honour fell with him, and now my life.

(V.iii.157–61)

Beatrice's change is as inevitable as the fulfillment of the puns which Christopher Ricks has pointed out in the play.[4] Chivalric "service" becomes sexual "service" (as in *Women Beware Women* mercantile "business" becomes sexual "business") because the one meaning of the word is carried in the other; and in the same way is Beatrice's lust and dishonor a realization of what was inherent in her supposed love for Alsemero. Her moral degeneration, a process to a great extent dramatized in the word play, is, like the word play, a fulfillment of latent meaning.

There are many sources which can explain the manifest similarities among Middleton's plays, not least the apprenticeship in the coterie theater which left its mark upon his whole career, but one which is a paradigm for all the others and which has not been adequately appreciated is the dramaturgy of the morality play. As has already been men-

---

[4] "The Moral and Poetical Structure of *The Changeling*," *EC*, X (1960), 290–306; and "Word-Play in *Women Beware Women*," *RES*, XII (1961), 238–50.

tioned in connection with Jonson's comical satires, the morality, designed to represent the battle between virtue and vice within the soul of man by means of personification, increasingly focussed upon the gulling intrigue of the Vice against the figure of mankind. In the later moralities the Vice becomes a sardonic stage manager, who with grotesque hilarity manipulates and leads men to their damnation. He succeeds and his intrigue is successful because allegorically he is not outside mankind but within him. His characteristic aggression and deceit, as well as his homiletic showmanship, represent the inner processes of sin itself. His victory over mankind is thus a dramatization of man embracing the folly or destruction that is within his own nature, and the dynamics of his intrigue becomes at once an instrument of theatrical vitality (often self-conscious) and of inherent moral meaning.[5]

It is precisely this union of self-conscious theatrical intrigue and intrinsic moral definition which we find in Middleton's plays. It is most obvious in the early city comedies, where it blends easily with many of the characteristics of comical satire. Quomodo, Fitsgrave, Follywit, Witgood, and the Phoenix are all standard satirical commentators and at the same time, though in different ways, analogous to the Vice figure. They are all gullers whose comic delight is a function of the human weaknesses which they expose and upon which they capitalize, and like their predecessors, they are self-conscious playmakers whose plots are themselves emblems of human folly or vice. Quomodo's purposes are malign and he is in that respect closer to the Vice in tone as well as in intention; the others, though in varying degrees self-interested, are more gracious and they create plots which reflect their high spirits. But all of them are at once stage directors and commentators who help create and control the response to their respective plays, their roles both reflecting and combining theatrical self-consciousness and moral and satiric purpose.

In the tragicomedies, as later in the tragedies, the intrigues are both more serious and more immediately reminiscent of the moralities. In *A Fair Quarrel*, Jane, who is unmarried and pregnant, enlists the aid of a physician to give her "deliverance" from her problem. She is punningly flippant about her condition, even arrogant, until the physician asks to be paid "in the same quality / That I to you tendred, thats love for love" (III.ii.77–78). When she persists in misunderstanding his intentions, he reminds her not to make herself "ignorant / In what you know; you have tane forth the lesson / That I would read to you" (ll. 86–88). When she still refuses to understand him, he makes himself undeniably clear:

[5] See Spivack, *Shakespeare and the Allegory of Evil*, pp. 96–205.

Phy. Pray you mistake me not, indeed I love you.
Jane. Indeed? what deed?
Phy. The deed that you have done.
Jane. I cannot believe you.
Phy. Believe the deed!

(ll. 96–100)

As with her descendant, Beatrice Joanna, language as well as action compel Jane to recognize that she has become the deed's creature, and as in the later case the whole of the intrigue dramatizes a psychomachic process: her arrogance representing the blindness of lust, and the unexpected fulfillment of her puns its inevitable retribution. There is a similar portrait in *The Witch*, of Francisca, who is also pregnant, and whose brazen ironies— in puns and asides—depict both the desperation of her situation and the process of degradation which is its consequence. The Fletcherian resolutions of both plays prevent either woman's predicament from being pursued to its logical catastrophe (Jane, repentant, exposes herself and the physician; Francisca is simply forced to marry her seducer), but nonetheless the major burden of their characterizations, as of many others in the tragicomedies, is upon the ways in which their actions as well as thoughts enact the viciousness to which they are inclined. They are not allegorical characters, but something like an abstraction informs them.

Middleton's tragedies in some respects resemble the moralities even more explicitly than do the comedies and tragicomedies. The following speech from *Hengist*, for example, could as easily have come from the *Psychomachia*, the fount of the morality play:

>   the mischeifes
> That peoples a lost honour: oh they're infinite
> For as at a small Breach in towne or Castle
> When one has entrance, a whole Army followes,
> In Woman, so abusively once knowne,
> Thousandes of sins has passadge made with one:
> Vice comes with tropes, and they that entertaine
> A mighty potentate must receive his traine.
>   (IV.ii.272–79)

The speech not only describes Roxena, to whom it is applied, but also Bianca and Beatrice Joanna, whose downfalls are also represented as capitulations to vice and sin. Bianca is not entirely responsible, initially, for her first breach, but once the Duke enters, the army of vices within herself follows relentlessly, manifesting itself in the materialism of her imagery, in her lust, her contempt for Leantio and his mother, and in her final role as a murderess. Beatrice admits the first sin herself, and the major interest of *The Changeling* lies in the spectacle of the vices that, one by one, troop in to besiege and ultimately destroy the castle of her soul—a spectacle which is dramatized not only in her gradually increasing love for Deflores, but in imagery that associates the abuse of her soul with the abuse of her father's castle.[6]

The whole relationship between Beatrice and Deflores, indeed, has psychomachic overtones. Deflores has many of the characteristics of the Vice. He is a sinister clown, very fond of telling the audience what he is doing, both openly in asides and, less overtly, in insidious puns, and he is a master stage-manager and intriguer. His ugliness and his lust make him human, but both are also sufficiently exaggerated to make him seem an example, if not a personification, of the ideas of moral ugliness and lust. Moreover, he succeeds so superbly with Beatrice because his relationship with her is conceived, at least in part, as one between the Vice and his victim. Deflores has too much life and vitality to be reduced to an abstraction, but he is nonetheless a tempter who is incestuously tied to Beatrice in a way that suggests that he has become a part of her, as she of him. Their relationship is not unlike that of Iago and Othello, and as in Shakespeare, its progress represents a kind of psychomachia of the soul's gradual surrender to vice. Beatrice herself seems to realize this when she tells her father that her fate always hung upon Deflores, " 'mongst things corruptible, / I ne're could pluck it from him, my loathing / Was Prophet to the rest, but ne're beleeved" (V.iii.158–60). Alsemero in fact calls Deflores and Beatrice "twins of mischief," (V.iii. 145) and though Deflores, like the old Vice, feels no remorse, while Beatrice feels alienated and ashamed, they both end by denouncing each other, like Hersus and Vortiger in *Hengist*, and like all the sinners whose mutual destruction in the finale of *Women Beware Women* is the final seal of kinship in sin, the final emblem of sin's inevitable self-consumption.

Middleton's tragedies are hardly allegories, of course, and their characters, which were played by adults rather than boys, are, even more than those in his comedies, "men and women of the time." There is thus reason to stress their psychological insight, as most critics have done, as long as we do not allow an emphasis upon a modern understanding of psychology and personality to falsify Middleton's dramaturgy. The judgment made upon Quomodo, as upon all the other characters in Middleton's plays, "Thou art thine owne affliction," is indeed a striking statement of a basic premise of Freudian psychology, but it is also, one

---

[6] See T. B. Tomlinson, *A Study of Elizabethan and Jacobean Tragedy* (Cambridge, 1964), pp. 192–208.

must remember, an assumption of the Bible, and the Bible has assumptions and values which Freud does not have. Though the morality plays demonstrate great insight into human behavior, their psychological insight is moral, not naturalistic, and their method is allegorical, not realistic, and a failure to appreciate how these distinctions may apply to Middleton's plays can lead to distortions and misinterpretations.

One distortion is to regard Middleton's interest in intrigue as a debasement of his moral concern,[7] when, as we have seen, quite the opposite is the case. The intrigues in all his plays are the means by which Middleton apprehends and realizes his moral insights in dramatic form, because, as in the moralities, the relationship between the guller and the gulled itself constitutes a moral definition. And this is as true of Middleton's comedies as of his tragedies: the relationships between Quomodo and his victim, Deflores and his, or Livia and hers, are comparable, though they are exploited for purposes which differ according to the different genres.

A related distortion is to regard the evident fantastic strain in Middleton's drama—the exaggerations, the grotesqueries, the farce—as a symptom of his inability to reconcile an amoral theatrical vitality with stringent Calvinistic judgments.[8] Not only is this opposition a false one, as we have observed, but the accusation indicts Middleton for betraying dramatic premises which he never intended to follow. His plays are filled with episodes or situations which are preposterous or incredible: Harebrain in *A Mad World, My Masters* listening patiently outside the door of the room in which his wife is being seduced; Allwit in *A Chaste Maid in Cheapside* becoming rhapsodic about how blessed and profitable his cuckoldom is; Roxena in *Hengist* taking an oath of virginity; Beatrice in *The Changeling* taking a potion to test virginity; the Duchess and Amoretta in *The Witch* falling in love because of a magic ribbon; the same Duchess, and Beatrice in *The Changeling*, and the Duke in *Women Beware Women*, believing that murder is no dishonour, though fornication is. With enough effort most of these episodes, and others like them, can be made to conform to the laws of psychology and probability, and those that cannot can either be dismissed as the consequence of Middleton's subjection to his audience or blamed on Rowley. But the real point is that for better or for worse they are often a reflection of the characteristic conceptions and techniques of the morality play. Beatrice's almost incredible insensitivity to Deflores's puns, for example, can be understood as a seventeenth-century adapta-

---

[7] See, e.g., Samuel Schoenbaum, *Middleton's Tragedies* (New York, 1955), p. 150, and "Middleton's Tragicomedies," *MP*, LIV (1956), 7–19.

[8] This tends to be R. B. Parker's bias in "Middleton's Experiments with Comedy and Judgment," in *Jacobean Theatre*, eds. Brown and Harris, pp. 179–199.

tion of what in the older morality would have been a personification of moral blindness.[9] Similarly, the virginity potion or the love ribbon are unbelievable or merely melodramatic only if we fail to recognize that in a fashion common to morality play drama they are visible abstractions, designed to figure forth morally symbolic action. Indeed, the peculiar mixture of realistic and unrealistic in Middleton's plays, of near-farce and seriousness, close observation and extravagant distortion, far from being a sign of either moral or artistic confusion, is often the signature of an entirely coordinated moral and dramatic purpose.

The most important benefit of referring to the morality tradition in interpreting Middleton's plays, however, is that it helps us understand the ironic tone which seems to lie at the heart of his work. Some of his ironic practices we have already touched upon. The retributive patterns of action and characterization which run through the plays are of course profoundly ironic: it is virtually Middleton's first law of moral dynamics that every foolish or vicious action has its equal and opposite reaction. Both the guller and the gulled are subject to it: there is no folly or vice which is not precisely repaid in kind, no evil which does not bring its own destruction. A perfect symmetry governs Middleton's better plays —fearful in the tragedies and delightful in the comedies, but always ironically inexorable. In the motivations of the characters, as well as in their actions, there is an absolute conservation of the energy of sin of which we are made acutely conscious, so that nothing the characters feel or say or do exists apart from the ironic awareness about them which we share with the dramatist himself. This awareness also affects the tragi-comedies, where it is, however, often diluted by arbitrary turns of action.

Such an awareness, of course, is inevitable in the morality play. Usually a presenter introduces the drama and tells the audience what is going to happen, and the chief action of the play, the intrigue, is carefully and constantly explicated by the Vice (or vices). Both the presenter and the Vice act as surrogates for the dramatist, establishing direct contact with the audience and enabling it to see beyond and above the immediate action. The Vice's habitual clowning with deadly serious matters is also of obvious importance in generating this detachment. In addition, since all the characters in the moralities are purely personifications and the action is never intended to be naturalistic, the ironies of mankind's behavior can be made evident by direct homiletic lectures, symbolic props, symbolic episodes, and rather explicit verbal ironies.

The irony in Middleton's plays, though no less intense, is not nearly

---

[9] For a discussion of the pervasive imagery of blindness in the play, see Edward Engelberg, "Tragic Blindness in *The Changeling* and *Women Beware Women*," *MLQ*, XXIII (1962), 20–28.

so straightforward. The characters are not simply personifications, their actions not simply allegorical. There is no presenter, and the vices are only in partial control of the action since they are themselves subject to it; they have human motivations of their own. Quomodo is greedy as well as an emblem of greed, the physician, Deflores, and Livia are lustful as well as symbols of the lust that is in others. Middleton is obviously not writing for a medieval audience, and however much morality play conceptions govern the characterizations and the relationships between characters, the conventions with which they are portrayed are those of the seventeenth-century stage. Middleton's plays are self-sustaining images of recognizable human beings, and the irony which Middleton sees at their heart he expresses from within, without disrupting the semi-realistic illusion.

The balance is exceptionally delicate. In his early city comedies Middleton was helped in achieving it, I think, by the conditions of performance in the coterie theater. Its peculiar blend of engagement and detachment at the least offered him analogies for making morality conceptions and techniques viable on a semi-realistic stage and may even have played a leading part in creating his interest in those conceptions and techniques in the first place. Actual moralities were staged by the children's companies when they first resumed performances in 1599 and 1600,[10] and their direct influence upon the companies seems probable. But in any event Middleton's comedies exploit the effects of coterie preciosity for moral purpose.

A Mad World, My Masters offers several particularly brilliant examples. Throughout the play Follywit writes, directs, and acts in a variety of plays within plays performed for the benefit of his uncle. In one of these plays Follywit dresses up as his uncle's whore before our eyes, making appropriate ironic comments in the process about the moral implications of what he is doing:

Folly-w. Come, come, thou shalt see a woman quickely made up here.
Leift.   But that's against kind Captaine, for they are alwaies long a making ready.
Folly-w. And is not most they doe against kind, I prethee? to lie with their Horse-keeper, is not that against kind? to weare half moons made of anothers haire, is not that against kind? to drinke downe a man, she that should set him up, pray is not that monstrously against kind now? nay over with it, Lieftenant, over with it, ever while

---

[10] See e.g., *The Contention of Liberality and Prodigality*, a Chapel play performed in 1601, as well as Marston's *Histriomastix* (1598–99). See also J. B. Leishman, *The Three Parnassus Plays* (London, 1949), p. 45; and Finkelpearl, *John Marston*, pp. 119–24.

you live put a womans clothes over her head: *Cupid* plaies best at
blind-man buff.

(III.iii.95–106)

Follywit associates the deception of theatrical costuming—which we see
enacted—with the deception of lust and whoredom. The scene is high-
spirited, of course, and hardly serious; but immediately following is a
scene in which Penitent Brothel is accosted by a devil in the shape of a
succubus of Mistress Harebrain, and the succubus is clearly analogous
to Follywit's unnatural transvestite role. Penitent, moreover, makes the
same points about lust in a straightforward and homiletic soliloquy as
Follywit does in flippant jests. Immediately after the scene with Penitent, Follywit appears in the disguise of the whore at his uncle's house,
gulls both his uncle and his uncle's servant (who propositions him!)
and draws a moral from the whole escapade: "Who keepes a Harlot
tell him this from me, / He needes nor theefe, disease, nor enemy"
(IV.iii.53–54). The somber tone of Penitent's soliloquy is perhaps dis-
crepant,[11] but otherwise this entire sequence of scenes is quite coherent
and presents a fine illustration of how Middleton exploits theatrical
self-display as a means of developing moral insights.

Another scene which demonstrates this process, this time seamlessly,
is the one in which Follywit produces his last play for his uncle. Disguised now as players, Follywit and his lieutenants[12] propose to enter-
tain Sir Bounteous and his guest with a comedy called "The Slip." Sir
Bounteous makes some comments about players: "now up & now
downe, they know not when to play, where to play, nor what to play,
not when to play for fearful fools, where to play for Puritane fooles, nor
what to play for criticall fooles" (V.i.31–34); and Follywit is distinguished as the "best Actor" in the company, with the "greatest share"
in its stock. At the same time Frank Gullman, now Follywit's wife, enters as Sir Bounteous's guest and he accuses her of robbing him, which
she naturally denies, since it was Follywit disguised as his whore who
had robbed him. Follywit then asks to borrow Sir Bounteous's watch
and chain as props for his part, and the play begins. Frank Gullman says
if she were not married she

could finde in my heart to fall in love with that Player now, and send for
him to a supper; I know some i' th' towne that have done as much, and

---

[11] See Standish Henning, introduction to *A Mad World, My Masters* (Lincoln,
Neb., 1965), pp. xiii–xiv.

[12] Like the old Vice, both Follywit and Quomodo are accompanied by their
lieutenants: Follywit by Ancient Hoboy and Lieutenant Mawworm, Quomodo by
Shortyard and Falselight.

there tooke such a good conceypt of their parts into 'th two-penny roome, that the Actors have bin found ith morning in a less compasse then their Stage, tho twere nere so full of gentlemen.

(V.ii.34–40)

Follywit meanwhile has concluded the prologue which was also intended to conclude the play: "The play being calld the Slip, I vanish too" (V.ii.28), but he faces a sudden crisis because a constable has apprehended his fellow "actors" and is returning to the house with them. In a master stroke, Follywit then assumes the part of a justice, abuses the constable and has him bound to a chair on stage. He and his lieutenants then flee and eventually Sir Bounteous and the rest of his audience discover what has happened:

Sir Bo. Give me leave, give me leave, why art not thou the Constable i'th comedy?
Const. Ith comedy? why I am the constable i'th commonwealth, sir.

(V.ii.168–71)

Follywit returns "*in his owne shape*" and kneels to ask his uncle's blessing, saying, "This showes like kneeling after the play" (V.ii.200). Shortly afterwards his playing is exposed as the alarm on his uncle's watch rings in his pocket—"Have I scapt the Constable to be brought in by the watch?" (V.ii.252)—and he learns that his wife is the very whore whom he himself had once played. Sir Bounteous draws the moral in lines we have already cited: "Who lives by cunning marke it, his fates cast, / When he has guld all, then is himself the last" (V.ii.298–99).

The final effect of the actors upon actors in this scene, and plays upon plays, is to underscore the confusion, at once entertaining and significant, of play-acting and being. As in Jonson's comical satires, all the characters are revealed as actors, sometimes playing roles that deceive others, almost always playing roles that deceive themselves. They are all children acting the parts of adults, players in the larger comedy of human folly in which even the constable of the commonwealth has a part. As in Jonson's plays also, Middleton combines this theatrical self-consciousness with devices of the morality so that one becomes an expression of the other. Follywit is for most of *A Mad World* a kind of Vice who, like his predecessors, is a writer and director of plays whose intrigues both represent folly and are animated by it. Follywit, of course, is more gracious than his predecessors, and because he is himself susceptible to the weaknesses upon which he plays, he is also more human, but the end result of his characterization as well as of the intrigues

which he governs is to cauterize our sympathies and to compel us to remain stringently conscious of the ironic economy of human foolishness.

The same kind of stringent economy and detachment determines
the effect of Middleton's tragedies. (The tragicomedies pose special
problems in this respect to which we will return.) We have already seen
the community of irony demonstrated in the comparison between the
speeches of Quomodo and Leantio, and a comparison of whole scenes
illustrates the similarities of conception and effect even more clearly.
Consider, for example, the scene in *A Mad World, My Masters* (III.ii)
in which Harebrain listens outside a door as "the flesh draws nie her
end" and the one in *Women Beware Women* (II.ii) in which the
mother plays chess as her daughter-in-law is being seduced—both celebrated scenes, and equally typical of their respective plays. The first is
comically outrageous. The substance of the scene lies in the *doubles
entendres* of the Courtesan's speeches, and of Harebrain's responses
to them:

Curtiz. Pray sit downe, there's a low stoole, good Mistris *Harebraine*, this
was kindly done; huh, give me your hand; huh, alas how cold you
are: ev'n so is your husband, that worthy wise Gentleman; as com-
fortable a man to woman in my case, as ever trod—huh—shooe
leather, love him, honour him, sticke by him, hee lets you want
nothing, that's fit for a woman; and to be sure on't, he wil see himselfe that you want it not.
Hareb. And so I doe yfaith, tis right my humour.

(III.ii.191–99)

The courtesan makes further *doubles entendres*, which Harebrain mag-
nifies by his reaction, and the irony is maintained to the end, when
Harebrain greets his wife as she emerges from the room:

Hareb. Welcome sweete wife, alight upon my lip, never was hower spent
better.
Wife. Why, were you within hearing sir?
Hareb. I that I was yfaith, to my great comfort; I deceivd you there wife,
ha, ha;
I doe intreat thee, nay conjure thee wife
Upon my love, or what can more be said?
Oftner to visit this sicke maid.
Wife. Be not so fierce, your will shal be obaide.
Hareb. Why then I see thou lov'st me.

(ll. 251–59)

There are several interesting things about this scene. First, though it
is hardly homiletic in its immediate effect, it is, in Middleton's usual

fashion, inherently moral in its conception. For the comedy is not that Harebrain is cuckolded, but that he cuckolds himself. His jealousy has created the conditions of his wife's seduction and precipitated it: he brings her to the assignation and is gulled entirely through his own vanity and folly. He not only deserves what he gets, but, as in the moralities, what he gets is a natural extension and expression of his own character. Secondly, we experience these ironies through devices of situation and language which give us perspective on the action and keep us at some distance from it. Children acting the seduction scene obviously provide one perspective. The Courtesan's mock conversation provides another, since it is in fact a commentary which explains to the audience what is at once so funny and so just about what is happening. The *doubles entendres*, the Courtesan's intentional ones as well as Harebrain's unintentional ones, function in the same way. Moreover, both the word play and the commentary have the effect of making us a party not only to the Courtesan's playmaking, but to Middleton's as well. Finally, the scene is significant because both in its overall conception and in its particular use of the commentator and of verbal irony, it is entirely typical of coterie satiric comedy.

The scene in *Women Beware Women* is naturally more serious—more serious in its consequences, more serious in its representation. Lust is portrayed as adult viciousness, not childish folly. Bianca is an unwilling victim, at least at first, and we see what is happening to her as we do not see what happens to Mistress Harebrain. But the similarities between the two scenes, in both shape and texture, are equally remarkable. Livia, like the Courtesan, is the true focus of the scene: she directs it, acts in it, and comments upon it. Where the Courtesan's audience was Harebrain, hers is the Mother, and where the medium of the Courtesan's commentary were the *doubles entendres* of the pretended conversation, hers is the sustained *double entendre* of the chess game.

> Liv.   Come Widow, look you Lady, here's our business;
>   Are we not well employ'd think you! an old quarrel
>   Between us, that will never be at an end.
> Bran. No, and methinks there's men enough to part you (Lady).
> Liv.   Ho! but they set us on, let us come off
>   As well as we can, poor souls, men care no farther.
>
>   .   .   .   .   .
>
>   here take these keys,
>   Shew her the Monument too, and that's a thing
>   Every one sees not; you can witness that Widow.
>
>   .   .   .   .   .
>
>   After a game or two, w'are for you Gentlefolks.

Guard. We wish no better seconds in Society
       Then your discourses, Madam, and your partners there.
Moth. I thank your praise, I listen'd to you Sir;
       Though when you spoke, there came a paltry Rook
       Full in my way, and choaks up all my game:
                        Exit Guardiano & Brancha.
Liv. Alas poor Widow, I shall be too hard for thee.
Moth. Y'are cunning at the game, I'll be sworn (Madam).
            (II.ii.267–72, 281–84, 294–300)

From this point forward the chess game directly parallels Bianca's seduction. Livia checks the Mother's white king, and on the upper stage
Guardiano draws a curtain to discover the Duke to Bianca. The Duke
overcomes Bianca, and immediately after they exit from the upper
stage, Livia comments:

Liv. Did not I say my Duke would fetch you over (Widow)?
Moth. I think you spoke in earnest when you said it (Madam).

Shortly after, Livia begins to bring the game to an end:

Liv. The game's ev'n at the best now; you may see Widow
       How all things draw to an end.
Moth. Ev'n so do I Madam.
       .   .   .   .
Liv. Has not my Duke bestir'd himself?
Moth. Yes faith Madam; h'as done me all the mischief in this Game.
Liv. H'as shew'd himself in's kinde.
Moth. In's kinde, call you it?
       I may swear that.
Liv. Yes, faith, and keep your oath.
           (ll. 393–94; 414–15; 420–24)

The scene then closes with the return of Bianca, bitter, "acquainted"
now with sin, and a conscious party to the ironies which surround her:

Moth. You have not seen all since sure?
Bran. That have I Mother,
       The Monument and all: I'm so beholding
       To this kinde, honest, curteous Gentleman,
       You'ld little think it (Mother) show'd me all,
       Had me from place to place, so fashionably;
       The kindness of some people, how't exceeds?
       'Faith, I have seen that I little thought to see,
       I'th morning when I rose.

Moth.   Nay, so I told you
        Before you saw't, it would prove worth your sight.
        I give you great thanks for my daughter Sir,
        And all your kindness towards her.
Guard. O good Widow!
        Much good may do her; forty weeks hence, y'faith.
                                              (ll.455–66)

There are base notes in this scene which we never hear in *A Mad World*. We witness the terrible insinuation of the Duke's rhetoric and power and we must sympathize with Bianca's corresponding helplessness. But on the other hand our sympathy finally contributes to a more heightened sense of irony which is comparable to that of the comedies. For however much we sympathize with Bianca we see also that the seduction is only another variety of chess game, and the very humanity of the pieces makes it not less a game but more, since their human inadequacy is what finally makes their moves so predictable and inexorable. The stakes of the game are higher, but it is the same game that is played in the comedies, as well as in the moralities, and it is played and represented in much the same way. In the tragedy there is more emotion, more sympathetic human substance, but the ironic pattern is similar and so is our apprehension of it. We see the comic inevitability of the seduction of Mistress Harebrain through the high spirited *doubles entendres* of the Courtesan, we see the tragic inevitability of the seduction of Bianca through the insidious *doubles entendres* of Livia: in neither case are emotional sympathies allowed to obscure our apprehension of the moral inevitability of what happens. The chess game, with Livia's comments upon it, guarantees such a dispassionate apprehension not only directly, by overtly instructing us how we are to understand the seduction, but also indirectly, by interposing itself between the seduction and us. The game functions not as a metaphor which involves us more deeply in the action, but as a simile which ensures our distance from it; and the ironic effect this distance creates is reminiscent of both the moralities and the satiric drama of the coterie. Livia is at once Middleton's presenter and his satiric commentator, and the action she directs and comments upon is at once an abstraction of human behavior and a conscious theatrical demonstration of it.

One further comparison between Middleton's tragedy and his coterie comedy may serve to show the identity of their ironic methods and their common heritage in dramaturgical conceptions of the morality play. One of the most characteristic scenes in Middleton's early comedies as well as in the coterie theater in general is the scene in *Michaelmas Term* (II.iii) in which Easy signs away his money and his land. The action is twice refracted before we are allowed to respond to it: first in the constant asides of the gullers: "Now my sweet Shortyard,—now the hungry fish begins to nibble: one end of the worme is in his mouth yfaith" (II.iii.223–25); and secondly in the presence and occasional comments of Quomodo's wife Thomasine, who stands on the upper stage observing the proceedings:

> Why stand I here (as late our gracelesse Dames
> That found no eyes) to see that Gentleman
> Alive, in state and credite executed,
> Helpe to rip up himselfe, do's all he can,
> Why am I wife to him that is no man?
> I suffer in that Gentlemans confusion.
>
> (ll. 226–31)

The final effect of the concatenation of asides and of Thomasine's comments is a rich counterpoint of ironies with a corresponding richness and subtlety in our response. On the one hand we experience the straightforward irony of Easy's eagerness to play his part in a play which Quomodo has contrived and is directing with evident delight; and on the other hand we experience the irony of the unseen audience to that play responding in a way which Quomodo hardly intended and which, even at this point, we suspect may eventually put him on stage himself. The end result is that interest and detachment are created in equal proportion, and we are involved in the action at the same time that we are carefully kept apart from it. Easy gains our interest—perhaps even our sympathy—but without the slightest diminution of our ironic awareness of his situation or of him.

Essentially the same dramatic process is at work in Middleton's tragedies. At the center of the magnificent banquet scene in *Women Beware Women* (III.ii), for example, is a comparable ironic awareness, deeper, wider, and more compassionate, but not different in kind. The scene is a tissue of asides and ironic perspectives. Leantio is given a captainship, and in an aside finds some comfort in being a cuckold: "I'm like a thing that never was yet heard of, / Half merry, and half mad" (III.ii.52–53). At the same moment Livia notices Leantio for the first time and feeling the "power of love" for him, is confident that she has "enough to buy me my desires" (ll. 61, 63). The Ward makes a bestial speech about Isabella. The Duke toasts Bianca, and Leantio makes the speech, in an aside, which we quoted earlier: "So, so; / Here stands the poor theif now that stole the treasure" (ll. 87 ff.). Fabricio and the Duke discuss the marriage of Isabella and the Ward, Fabricio treating his daughter entirely as chattel; Bianca makes asides about poor Isabella's fate, and Leantio in turn makes bitter asides about Bianca. Music is played, Leantio exclaims, "Oh that Musick mocks me," and immediately afterwards Livia says in an aside: "I am as dumb to any language now / But Loves, as one that never learn'd to speak" (ll. 135–37). Isabella sings a song of the hard chance of a woman falling to a fool's use; the Ward makes an idiotic comment. Fabricio asks the Ward to dance with Isabella; he refuses and gives the honor to Hippolito, who tells Isabella:

> Come my life's peace, I have a strange office on't here,
> 'Tis some mans luck to keep the joys he likes
> Conceal'd for his own bosom; but my fortune
> To set 'em out now, for anothers liking.
>
>   (ll. 193–96)

Then more conversation—between the Duke and Fabricio, between the Guardian and Bianca, between the Duke and Bianca—and constant asides by Leantio about Bianca. The Ward and Isabella dance, "*he ridiculously imitates* Hippolito" (l. 227). The Duke and Bianca leave and Leantio cries out in pain as Livia looks on:

> *Lean.* As long as mine eye saw thee
>   I half enjoy'd thee.
> *Liv.*   Sir?
> *Lean.* Canst thou forget
>   The dear pains my love took, how it was watch't
>   Whole nights together, in all weathers for thee,
>   Yet stood in heart more merry then the tempests
>   That sung about mine ears, like dangerous flatterers
>   That can set all their mischeif to sweet tunes;
>   And then receiv'd thee from thy fathers window,
>   Into these arms at midnight, when we embrac'd
>   As if we had been Statues onely made for't,
>   To shew arts life, so silent were our comforts,
>   And kiss'd as if our lips had grown together!
> *Liv.*   This makes me madder to enjoy him now.
>
>   (ll. 251–63)

By the end of the scene, after several similarly pointed ironic juxta-positions of asides and speeches (Leantio, for example, says that "This cannot be but of some close Bauds working" [l. 267] and then turns to speak to Livia), Leantio gives up his "life's wealth" and Livia, as we have seen, gets her wish:

> *Liv.*   Do but you love enough, I'll give enough.
> *Lean.* Troth then, I'll love enough, and take enough.
> *Liv.*   Then we are both pleas'd enough.
>
>   (ll. 375–77)

The richness of ironies in this scene is remarkable, even for Middleton, but the method of the scene is not. The characters are men and women of the time and are certainly moving (Leantio especially) in ways that neither morality personifications nor coterie actors are, but within and behind them are comparable dramatic premises. The tune that sings about the ears of all the characters and that drives them is the inexorable tune of human mortality and lust—the same tune that suffuses the moralities and coterie comedy—and the pervasive irony and the stylization of the music and dancing comprise Middleton's equivalent for the allegorical detachment of the moralities and the theatrical self-consciousness of coterie comedy. The endless counterpoint of asides and ironies eventually compose all the feelings and actions of the characters into a pattern as formal and prescribed as the music they play or the dances to which they move; and the music and the dances themselves, like the chess game earlier in the play, at once comment upon the action, abstract it, and compel us to keep ever conscious of the simultaneous symmetries of its substance and its design.

This is a symmetry, as we have seen, which is not uncommon in tragicomedy, where it is encouraged by a similarly acute and complex theatrical self-consciousness. It is therefore interesting that Middleton's tragicomedies should not be more successful than they are. As a group they resemble his tragedies more than his comedies. Like the tragedies they explore the dynamics of sin and like them too they use irony to cauterize our responses. All four of the major tragicomedies have characterizations that are reminiscent of the finer portraits of the tragedies. Jane in *The Fair Quarrel* and Francisca in *More Dissemblers Besides Women*, ancestors of Bianca as well as Beatrice Joanna, we have already mentioned. Lactantio in *More Dissemblers Besides Women* and Sebastian in *The Witch* are of the family of Leantio, the former a study of greed, the latter of desire. Sebastian, especially, is memorable for long soliloquies which, like Leantio's, deal with deprivation, loss, and spiritual emptiness. Other sinners in the plays, and particularly women like Eugenia in *The Old Law*, the Duchess in *The Witch*, and both Aurelia and the Duchess in *More Dissemblers Besides Women*, reveal the same kind of penetrating self-awareness and yet compulsive deterioration which marks the women in the tragedies. Not merely characterizations, moreover, but whole scenes and situations generate effects which are comparable to those of the tragedies. There are many scenes, in particular, which employ intense word play and concatenations of asides. The opening scene of *The Witch* is very like the banqueting scene in *Women Beware Women*, and in all the tragicomedies there are dialogues developing extended puns. The whole of *The Old Law* has something of the sense of a corrupt society which dominates *Women*

Beware Women. The Duke of Epire promulgates a law stipulating that men who have reached fourscore, and women threescore, must be put to death, and for a good part of the play Middleton concentrates upon the almost unreal avarice and mercilessness of the children who await or try to advance their parents' execution.

For all their power, however, these characters, scenes, and situations are essentially isolated and their effects often truncated by the overall designs of the plays in which they occur. The tragicomedies end happily, but in order that they do so Middleton has to resort to the baldest and most superficial contrivances. Knots are untied by casual misunderstandings or deceptions, confirmed sinners repent in an instant, and dead men come back to life without warning. The result is that the resolutions are not merely unconvincing in themselves, but deny the theatrical and moral logic of the strongest characters and scenes of the plays they conclude. In the process the integrity of intrigue and character which is the hallmark of Middleton's other plays (comedies as well as tragedies) is disturbed.

The immediate reason for this failure is probably Fletcher, whose influence is apparent in the declamations upon honor and dueling in *The Fair Quarrel*, in the improbable hypothesis that forms the premise of *The Old Law*, and in the radical peripeties of plot and Protean changes of character in all the plays. But the reason behind the reason, the reason that Middleton could not turn the Fletcherian model to advantage as Shakespeare did, is that his dramaturgy was simply not susceptible to that kind of exploitation of tragicomic form. His basic dramatic instincts were like Jonson's. He had neither Shakespeare's interest in the resolving epiphanies of *felix culpa* nor his capacity to explore the confrontation of tragic and comic extremes. Nourished by both the older Vice comedy and the satire of the contemporary coterie theater, the actions of Middleton's plays tend to be static and monochromatic. This is no doubt a limitation, but it is also the source of his peculiar power: a clarified and intense dispassion, as penetrating as it is ironic, without parallel in Jacobean drama.

VI

Webster

W EBSTER is probably the most controversial of Jacobean dramatists. There are critics who do not find any virtues in him and those who do cannot agree upon what they are. There is an especially radical split between those who prefer *The White Devil* and those who prefer *The Duchess of Malfi*, each group praising its choice for precisely the same reasons that the other condemns it. One critic sees an access of compassion in *The Duchess*, for example, where a second sees sentimentality, and the second sees an uncompromising objectivity in *The White Devil* where the first sees only sensationalism. As Moody Prior has observed,[1] such judgments seem finally to be a matter of taste, and no amount of argument is likely to affect them. A critic can only hope that his taste is good and that the distinctions he makes are not too invidious. My own preference—or prejudice—is for *The Duchess*.

In *The White Devil*, by his own admission, Webster drew heavily upon other men's work. In the preface to the play he cites the "full and haightned style of Maister *Chapman*: The labor'd and understanding workes of Maister *Johnson*: The no lesse worthy composures of the both worthily excellent Maister *Beamont*, & Maister *Fletcher*: And lastly (without wrong last to be named) the right happy and copious industry of M. *Shake-speare*, M. *Decker*, & M. *Heywood*."[2] The priority of place in this list goes to the three dramatists who were largely or entirely concerned with the private theater, and their influence is very apparent in Webster's play. There are several specific imitations of *Sejanus* in *The White Devil*;[3] the sentences which pervade the play, as well as the stoical positions often voiced in the sentences, seem directly attributable to Chapman's style; and the frequent radical changes in attitude of such characters as Vittoria, Monticelso, and Brachiano, as well as the contrived theatricalism of such scenes as Flamineo's feigned death, are

---

[1] *The Language of Tragedy* (New York, 1947), p. 120. For a discussion of the history of Webster criticism, see Don D. Moore, *John Webster and his Critics, 1617–1964* (Baton Rouge, La., 1966).

[2] References to the texts and act, scene, and line numbers of Webster's plays are to *The Complete Works of John Webster*, ed. F. L. Lucas, 4 vols. (London, 1927).

[3] See *The White Devil*, ed. John Russell Brown (Cambridge, Mass., 1962), p. 129.

clearly derived from the sensationalism of Fletcherian drama. Another evident coterie influence, which curiously Webster does not mention, is Marston, for whose *Malcontent* he had written the induction when the play was performed at the Globe in 1604 by the King's Men. Both the insistent satiric commentary of *The White Devil* and the commentators themselves (Flamineo especially) bear the mark of Marston's drama.

Webster, of course, also borrowed from public theater dramatists, including Shakespeare, who he assures us is "without wrong last to be named," but what distinguishes his debt to dramatists like Marston and Fletcher is that it goes beyond particular instances and affects his basic theatrical premises. Webster wrote a mongrel drama, as even his admirers acknowledge, and the critical problem is not in finding particular imitations or parallels—these abound—but in evaluating the extent to which he may be said to have assimilated them to his own distinctive style. The premises of the coterie theater, I think, were the most important stimuli in the creation of this style and thus provide the best means of understanding the rationale of the plays and of judging their success.

The White Devil's affinity to coterie dramaturgy is evident both in its pervasive satiric commentary and in its self-conscious theatricality. The presence of satiric commentary is obvious and overwhelming. Flamineo is the chief agent of this commentary. He is on stage in virtually every big scene of the play, and though he participates directly in the action of only a few of them, he makes comments upon all of them. Commentary, indeed, is Flamineo's principal form of action, defining both his character and his role, insofar as the two are separable. His comments range from aphoristic sententiae to full dress diatribes, and they fill the play. In any production, Flamineo tends to be the dominating figure, and his presence alone, as well as what he says, almost always affects our response to the characters and situations he observes. Like the commentators in many coterie plays, he stands partially outside the action, often interposing himself between it and us. Other characters in the play exercise a similar function. Both Francisco and Lodovico, for example, frequently act as satirical observers, Lodovico, somewhat in the fashion of Tourneur's Vindici, even providing a satiric framework for the play in the opening scene. Even the style of the play, with its proliferate sententiae, reflects the tendency to make us pay less attention to what is happening than to what is being said about what is happening.

The self-conscious theatricalism of *The White Devil* is in part related to this same tendency. To begin with, the commentary—especially Flamineo's—often compels us to regard characters as actors with essentially predetermined roles to play. A good example is the quarrel scene between Brachiano and Vittoria in the house of convertites (IV.ii).

Though the scene is ostensibly about the quarrel, its major focus is upon Flamineo's stage directions. As Vittoria begins to get as angry as Brachiano, Flamineo remarks, "Now, for two whirlewindes," (IV.ii.108) and when her tantrum has subsided, he directs her to "Turne to my Lord, good sister" (l. 137). When she refuses to play her part, he coaches Brachiano:

> What a damn'd imposume is a woman's will!
> Can nothing breake it? [*aside*] fie, fie, my Lord.
> Women are caught as you take Tortoises,
> Shee must bee turn'd on her backe. [*to Vittoria*] Sister, by
> this hand
> I am on your side. Come, come, you have wrong'd her
> What a strange credulous man were you, my Lord,
> To thinke the Duke of Florence would love her!
> Will any Mercer take anothers ware
> When once 't is tows'd and sullied? And yet, sister,
> How scurvily this frowardnesse becomes you!
> Yong Leverets stand not long; and womens anger
> Should, like their flight, procure a little sport;
> A full crie for a quarter of an hower;
> And then bee put to th' dead quat.
>   (ll. 152–65)

The scene then begins to assume the shape he desires and he continues his direction of it with asides to Brachiano:

> Hand her, my Lord, and kisse her: be not like
> A ferret to let go your hold with blowing.
>   .   .   .   .   .
> Now you are ith' way on't, follow't hard.
>   (ll. 170–71, 175)

and with bantering encouragement to Vittoria:

> Marke his penitence.
> Best natures doe commit the grossest faultes,
> When they're giv'n ore to jealosie; as best wine
> Dying makes strongest vinneger. Ile tell you;
> The Sea's more rough and raging than calme rivers,
> But nor so sweet nor wholesome. A quiet woman
> Is a still water under a great bridge.
> A man may shoot her safely.
>   (ll. 177–84)

The reconciliation is complete as Flamineo tells Brachiano to "Stop her mouth, with a sweet kisse, my Lord / So—now the tide's turned the ves-

sel's come about" (ll. 195–96). Flamineo's self-interest in the quarrel
(his career, if not his life, may hang upon its outcome) complicates our
reactions to his theatrical expertise, but we are nonetheless conscious
that it is theatrical and that the action he has directed is to be appreciated as a "scene" in both the dramatic and hysterical senses of the word.[4]

Flamineo stage-manages other scenes in much the same way. He studiously arranges the scenario for the assignation between Vittoria and
Brachiano (I.ii). He prepares Brachiano with sardonic comments on
the nature of women, gulls Camillo without mercy, deliberately treating
him as a cuckold in a comedy, and carefully explains to Vittoria how
she is to behave. Towards the end of the play, in his encounter with
Vittoria and Zanche (V.vi), he consciously stages opposite versions of
the same scene: the first consisting of his apparent murder by Vittoria
and Zanche, the second, of his murder of them. The third rendering,
which he has not planned, is his own murder, as well as Vittoria's, by
Lodovico.

Flamineo is also a conscious artificer of his own role. On at least three
occasions he explicitly explains his behavior in asides to the audience:

> I do put on this feigned Garbe of mirth,
> To gull suspicion.
>   (III.i.30–31)

because now I cannot counterfeit a whining passion for the death of my
Lady, I will faine a madde humor for the disgrace of my sister, and that will
keep off idle questions.
                                                         (III.ii.314–16)

> It may appear to some ridiculous
> Thus to talke knave and madman; and sometimes
> Come in with a dried sentence, stuft with sage.
> But this allowes my varying of shapes,
> *Knaves do grow great by being great mens apes.*
>   (IV.ii.242–46)

Finally, of course, Flamineo plays a role for a script which he has not
written, and he dies, by his own confession, "in a mist" (V.vi.260),
barely understanding either the "mase of conscience" (V.iv.115) within
himself, or the maze of human activity he has tried to direct. But his
failure does not diminish our consciousness of the play as a play, it simply includes Flamineo himself in the cast of that play.

Flamineo, moreover, is not the only means by which *The White*

---

[4] For a more conventional reading of this scene, see Travis Bogard, *The Tragic
Satire of John Webster* (Berkeley, Cal., 1955), pp. 108–09.

Devil calls attention to its own theatricalism. Other commentators or observers force us to step back from the action, and in scenes without commentators there are frequently other devices which sophisticate our response. At precisely the point, for example, when Flamineo stops managing the assignation scene, Cornelia enters to observe it, and we are compelled to watch her watching the lovers—not for a moment are we permitted to respond to Brachiano and Vittoria directly. Brachiano's death scene is similar: his agony is distilled (and indeed intensified) for us by our knowledge that his comforters are his oppressors and that his death scene has been staged by a cast of malevolent actors. The trial scene, too, we see as staged: both the judges, in their high-minded vindictiveness, and Vittoria, in her protestations of innocence, are playing roles. We tend to sympathize with Vittoria, but because she is an underdog, not because she is innocent, and in the last analysis we apprehend her passionate declarations of innocence as we do Evadne's "brave rage," as essentially declamatory.

It seems reasonable, therefore, to emphasize the conscious theatricalism of *The White Devil* as well as its satiric perspective, since the play itself insists on both so strongly. The real issue is what they mean. Those who are unsympathetic to *The White Devil* argue that, as in Fletcherian drama, its theatricalism expresses nothing but itself and that its insistent satiric commentary is finally only a means of absolving Webster from the necessity of committing himself to any organization or evaluation of his characters and their experiences.[5] Those who are sympathetic to the play maintain that the theatricalism and satiric commentary articulate precisely that difficulty in organizing or evaluating character and experience which it is Webster's desire to represent.[6]

John Russell Brown, who is the most perceptive of the play's admirers, argues in just this way. He contends that Webster's object is to present a world of moral and psychological relativity, if not chaos, and that the staginess and insistent intrusion of commentators between us and the action are among the natural expressions of such a vision. For him the preeminent realities of Webster's world are subconscious: the undisclosed and unknown motives, the "undertows" of character, the self-contradictions of virtue and vice, the "mist," to use Flamineo's word, of living itself; and these deeper realities are reached, he feels, through a theatrical strategy which deliberately inhibits our response to the surface of character or to a continuum of action and makes capital of the resul-

[5] See, e.g., M. C. Bradbrook, *Themes and Conventions of Elizabethan Tragedy* (Cambridge, 1935), p. 194; and T. B. Tomlinson, *A Study of Elizabethan and Jacobean Tragedy* (Cambridge, 1964), pp. 229–37.

[6] See, e.g., Clifford Leech, *John Webster, A Critical Study* (London, 1951), pp. 29–57; and Irving Ribner, *Jacobean Tragedy* (London, 1962), pp. 99–108.

tant conflicts between our moral judgments and our emotional sympathies.[7]

This kind of approach has the merit of arguing from, rather than against, the play's peculiar nature, and it is especially persuasive for a modern audience because contemporary theater has made this way of looking at life, not to mention plays, quite fashionable. The *angst* which allegedly afflicted all Jacobean dramatists is congenial to us, and their view of a tragic world in which heroism can only be defined existentially has our instinctive sympathy. The danger, of course, is that we may be reading our own preoccupations, and even more important, our own epistemology, into their plays. I think this may be the case with *The White Devil*.

To start with, it should be recognized that the kind of argument John Russell Brown presents cannot, by its very nature, be refuted. If the action is fragmented and stagey, the scenes unrelated, then this is the concept of action Webster wishes to dramatize; if the characters are histrionic, changeable and contradictory, this is the view of human personality he wishes to represent; and if our normal emotional and moral sympathies are frustrated by commentary and self-consciousness, in this way are we made to apprehend realities we do not normally see. Possibly so. But *The White Devil* may, after all, be a reflection of Webster's mistakes rather than of his intentions, and of his inadequacies as a dramatist rather than of his strengths. It is possible to make virtues of what are really limitations in a play and to interpret confusion in such a way as to make it seem expressive. And it is also quite possible to make a weak play look good on stage, so that even Brown's sensitive defense of the stageworthiness of *The White Devil* is not conclusive. That a play can be made to work is not necessarily an argument either for its merit or substance, as any capable performance of *The Maid's Tragedy*, or for that matter any tragicomedy of Beaumont and Fletcher, easily demonstrates.

There is really no way of breaking out of this circle and any analysis of Webster must finally be judged upon its tact and the usefulness and coherence of its particular insights. Perhaps my own reservations about *The White Devil* can be made most clear by comparing it to *The Malcontent*, since the two plays seem profoundly akin in their theatrical assumptions, yet very different in the results which they achieve. Though it "wants deaths," *The Malcontent*, like *The White Devil*, deals with a kind of secular hell. Both plays, in fact, have scenes which label themselves as hell: at Brachiano's death, Vittoria flees from the room in horror, crying: "O mee, this place is hell" (V.iii.179), and while

[7] Introduction to *The White Devil*, pp. xxxviii–lxii.

Malevole-Altofront is trying to seduce her in prison, Maria exclaims, "heere round about is hell" (V.ii.120). Both plays also create actions which are to be appreciated as deliberately grotesque comedies, performed in a maze: the jumbled ballet of Mendoza's unsuccessful intrigue against Ferneze's life (II.v), for example, is a perfect counterpart of the mock-suicide puppet show at the end of *The White Devil* (V.vi). The means of dramatizing these comedies of horror are also the same in both plays. Each has a central satiric commentator through whose sardonic eyes we see a disordered, atomistic world, and whose own character is the emblem of such a world. Each play has kaleidoscopic images of character and action; each is disposed to move from big scene to big scene with little logical connection. Finally—the common denominator of all the resemblances between them—each play compels us to keep partially outside of the action.

The difference between them, the critical difference, is that such distancing, with all its manifestations, serves an integrated and consistent purpose in *The Malcontent*, whereas in *The White Devil* it does not. In *The Malcontent*, as we have seen, Malevole's hegemony over the action and characters is quickly established: he is both the agent of all that happens and the means by which we interpret what happens; and as a result, however incoherent the discontinuities of the play may be in themselves, they are at least coherent and comprehensible as the projections of his character and his self-conscious role-playing. Moreover, the whole play comes to be apprehended as his vision, indeed, his creation, and consequently the pervasive effects of alienation, the sense that we are simultaneously being drawn into the action and pushed away from it, becomes a finely organic instrument of Marston's overall purpose. Our distance from the play and our awareness of its contrivance are at once the means by which we most fully experience Malevole's own ambivalent satiric position, *his* simultaneous involvement in, and detachment from, the action, and the means by which we experience the entire play as a play within a play, a play self-consciously poised between the horror and pain of reality and the absurdity and meaninglessness of a parodic make-believe. Theatrical self-consciousness is thus the perfect expression of both satire and tragicomedy in *The Malcontent* and the means by which the two are modulated and combined.

In *The White Devil*, by comparison, self-consciousness has no such poise and no such clarity of direction. There is, in the first place, more than one focus of interest in the play. Flamineo, though a dominating figure, must share the stage with a number of others—Vittoria most prominently—and unlike Malevole, is a victim as well as an agent in the action. As with Malevole, his sardonic attitudes drench the characters and action and affects our view of them, but in no sense does he have

Malevole's corresponding structural function: he is a tool, without real power, and ultimately the "night-piece" which the play limns is not his, but rather distractingly, Lodovico's. But even this evident structural dispersion is only a symptom, for what finally is most disturbing about *The White Devil* is that the multiple commentaries and the self-consciousness result in a dissipation of any moral perspective, and instead of deepening or clarifying the action—either for tragic or satiric point—they end, as in Fletcherian drama, by creating a succession of merely theatrical tableaux.

Individually, these tableaux have varying degrees of plausibility and capitalize upon their theatricality with varying degrees of power: the horror of Brachiano's death, for example, is amplified rather than diminished by our sense of theater in the scene, since the acting and staging of his tormentors are the natural expression of their malice, whereas the staginess of the trial scene, though in part understandable as a projection of the regulated hatred between the brothers and the lovers, ultimately reduces the scene to a declamatory debate in the Fletcherian mode.[8] But the real difficulty with the tableaux, the reason that even the powerful ones tend to be merely theatrical, is not that they have individual limitations, but that they do not function collectively. Aside from the broad assumption that life is hell, there is nothing resembling a coherent moral attitude in the play, and more important, nothing which enables us to integrate or organize its discontinuities of action and character. Unlike Jonson and Middleton, Webster does not have a sufficiently activated morality play framework to give significance to his picture of hell, and unlike Marston, he does not have the benefit of a consistent satiric or tragicomic control. His repeated verbal insistence upon the theme of "courtly reward and punishment" is evidence only of a conscious attempt to impose a satiric meaning which the play as a whole does not effectively dramatize. Anything can mean as much or as little in *The White Devil* as anything else. The grotesque travesty of the last rites in Brachiano's death scene depends for its effect upon a Christian orientation; Flamineo's, Vittoria's, and Zanche's deaths are horrible (and professedly heroic) precisely because they are Stoical and un-Christian. Vittoria's heroic defiance at her trial and at her death has the same value—dramaturgically and morally—as her hysterical tears with Brachiano, or her diabolical dream; and Flamineo's admiration of Vittoria's heroic death and his recognition of "compassion" and the "mase of conscience" within himself—a recognition to which admirers of the play cling very hard indeed—can ultimately only be understood

[8] For an analysis of the rhetoric of this scene, see H. Bruce Franklin, "The Trial Scene of Webster's *The White Devil* Examined in Terms of Renaissance Rhetoric," *SEL*, I (1961), 35–51.

as postures, without any more or any less meaning than his earlier Machiavellian cruelty.

It may be that this uncertainty or equivocation of "meaning" is deliberate, that Webster is interested in expressing the chaos of compulsive behavior and that self-conscious theatrical postures are the best means of representing such conflicts of impulse and will. New visions no doubt demand new modes of expression and the illogic and chaos of human action are certainly a legitimate province for a dramatist. But even in representing chaos a play itself must offer a coherent experience, and *The White Devil*, it seems to me, does not.

A final comparison, this time with *Macbeth*, reveals this inadequacy most clearly. *Macbeth* is like *The White Devil* in dealing with disintegrated wills and with a hellish world in which values are perverted and ambiguous. Unlike *The White Devil*, however, *Macbeth* provides the audience with the dramatic and moral orientation to understand and evaluate that ambiguity. The way in which this orientation works is perhaps best demonstrated in the scene between Malcolm and Macduff in England (IV.iii). In a long, curiously labored dialogue, Malcolm insists that he is not at all what he seems, that he is at least as evil as Macbeth, and that, given power, he will more than perpetuate the hell that is Scotland. Only after Macduff recoils in horror, and reacts with silent but expressive agony to the news of the murder of his wife and son, does Malcolm reveal that he has only been testing Macduff's motives and that his own seeming is false. The scene has often been cut in performances of the play, but is essential, for it establishes that there is an alternative to hell, a world outside of Scotland, and thereby restores to us the capacity to understand the corruption of values which Scotland has come to represent. Up to the point of their meeting, Macduff and Malcolm have been living a nightmare in which no man's motives were discernible, not even their own. Their almost ritualistic charade at once exorcises this nightmare and places it in perspective.[9] By acting out the dynamics of a hellish conversation they can resume a more normal one, and in the process give us the means of discriminating one from the other. We experience hell without being subject to its ultimate reduction of all human actions to varieties of emptiness and despair. We understand the damned, in other words, because we understand what they have lost.

There is no such understanding in *The White Devil*, and there is none because, as in Fletcherian drama, the play is ultimately about itself, a theatrical exhibit of hell rather than an exploration of it. This is an extreme judgment and is vulnerable to the charge of being reductive.

[9] For a relevant discussion of this scene, see Francis Fergusson, "*Macbeth* as an Imitation of an Action," *English Institute Essays 1951* (New York, 1952).

But the real issue is not that Webster relies on coterie methods in *The White Devil* but that he fails to do anything significant with them; and in this connection a comparison with *The Duchess of Malfi* is especially illuminating, for *The Duchess* uses much the same dramaturgy as the earlier play for effects which are more integrated and more penetrating.

At first sight *The Duchess of Malfi* seems to have more rather than fewer limitations than *The White Devil*. There does not appear to be any plausible motivation for Ferdinand and the Cardinal to oppose the Duchess's ever marrying again. Bosola's discovery that the Duchess has given birth is glaringly improbable and clumsy. At the end of Act II, after learning that the Duchess has had a child, Ferdinand vows "not to stir" till he knows "who leaps my sister"; the opening of Act III reveals that the Duchess has had two more children and that Ferdinand still has not stirred. The Duchess dies at the end of Act IV, and we appear to have one full act of anticlimax. The play is strewn with melodramatic tricks: wax figures, dancing madmen, a poisoned Bible, a lecherous, evil Cardinal, a mad, evil Duke, hooded executioners, sinister nighttime activities, mistaken stabbings. Its foci seem at least as dispersed as *The White Devil*'s, moving from one character to another and from one scene to another, and like the earlier play also, it has ostentatious apothegms and declamations at moments of high dramatic intensity. There seems, on the surface, no reason or way to experience the play as anything more than the hellish display of *The White Devil*.

But these difficulties either turn out to be more apparent than real in actual performance or to be comparatively undamaging. For *The Duchess of Malfi* takes root in Webster's imagination, and in ours, in a way that *The White Devil* never did. The methods and devices are the same, and the subject is the same—the "suburbs of hell" is the spiritual locale of both plays—but the crucial distinction is that in *The Duchess* they combine to form a unified play which provides us with at least an approach to a cohesive experience rather than with a series of sensations.

To begin with, *The Duchess of Malfi* has clear-cut moral guidelines of the kind that are almost entirely absent in *The White Devil*. The Duchess, however imprudent, is a good woman, and she truly loves Antonio; Antonio, in his turn, however much he fails to meet the exigencies of the situation that develops, is also good and is also truly in love. Bosola is a melancholy tool villain, but before he dies he changes, and for the better. Ferdinand is virulently evil, but his malevolence is morally explicable, at least, as both the cause and effect of his literal madness, and his brother, the Cardinal, suffers pricks of conscience and fear, if not remorse. The play as a whole opens with the establishment of a moral reference in Antonio's description of the virtuous court of France, and preserves this reference through the continued unsatirical comments of Delio.

The value of these moral distinctions is not that they prove some simple ethical lesson or elicit easy pathos, but that they organize the action and give us the bearings to comprehend and experience it. Largely because of them *The Duchess of Malfi* manages to create a structural as well as emotional focus and to bring together what remains divided in *The White Devil*. Except in an essentially circumstantial way, Flamineo's story and Vittoria's are separate in *The White Devil*. Flamineo is his sister's pandar, and the tool of her lover, but she comprises only a fraction of the satirical activity of his mind, which the play itself represents so fully, and she actually affects him once only, when she dies. Flamineo correspondingly, though always present when Vittoria is on stage, is only a part of her consciousness and has no discernible effect upon her at all. Neither makes any moral impression upon the other. Both are essentially insulated from one another, however congruent their positions or attitudes may be, and the attention we are required to give one of them frequently conflicts with, or distracts us from, the attention we are required to give the other. What distinguishes *The Duchess of Malfi* and altogether transforms it is that the comparable relationship between Bosola and the Duchess is different.

As with Vittoria, the Duchess's experience is the fulcrum of the play's action and its governing image; unlike Vittoria, the Duchess is a figure whose story and character are gradually developed and consistently sustained in a manner that increasingly engages our sympathies as well as our interest. The engagement is not a simple one. As has often been pointed out, the imagery of the play alone creates undercurrents which qualify the surface of the Duchess's actions or feelings.[10] Her betrothal scene, for example, is pervaded by ambivalent tones of rashness and love and by verbal anticipations of another kind of chamber which awaits her, and the prison scene itself presents a complex of ironic counterpoints to her despair and suffering. But the effect of all these devices of irony and counterpoint is that we are moved closer to the Duchess at the same time that we are made to keep some distance from her; and our simultaneous awareness of her love and of her folly only increases our capacity for compassion, because, as in Shakespearian drama, we are able to be sympathetic without losing our judgment and to feel pity without being sentimental. By the time the Duchess cries out, "I am Duchess of Malfi still," we can accept her statement as a meaningful act of self-definition and endurance, rather than as a mere theatrical gesture, be-

[10] See, e.g., Hereward T. Price, "The Function of Imagery in Webster," *PMLA*, LXX (1955), 717–39.

cause we can understand and sympathize with the character it defines; and all the concatenations of horror in the scene—unmatched in intensity by anything in *The White Devil*—all its madness and grotesqueness, are at least made comprehensible by the clarity and depth of our compassion.

The Duchess, however, is not alone in creating this compassion. Equally and crucially important is Bosola, for Bosola, the malcontent and cynic, responds not merely to the Duchess but to her whole experience in prison, and is transformed by it. At the very outset of the scene he attests to the nobility with which the Duchess is suffering: "a behaviour so noble, / As gives a majestie to adversitie" (IV.i.6–7), he tells Ferdinand, and any accent of exaggeration in the phrase is belied by Bosola's character. Later, after he protests against Ferdinand's "cruelty" and refuses to see the Duchess again in his own shape, Ferdinand remarks to him that "Thy pity is nothing of kin to thee" (IV.i.166). It had indeed not been, but its undeniable presence now both is explained by, and helps explain, the nobility of the Duchess's suffering. Throughout the remainder of the Duchess's ordeal, Bosola's pity is implied, and is paradoxically the more moving because he still seems compelled to keep to his part in killing her. When Ferdinand ungratefully casts him off after her death, and even his cynicism is not rewarded, Bosola's pity becomes enlarged into authentic self-recognition:

> What would I doe, we[r]e this to doe againe?
> I would not change my peace of conscience
> For all the wealth of Europe: She stirres; here's life:
> Returne (faire soule) from darkenes, and lead mine
> Out of this sencible Hell: She's warme, she breathes:
> Upon thy pale lips I will melt my heart
> To store them with fresh colour: who's there?
> Some cordiall drinke! Alas! I dare not call:
> So, pitty would destroy pitty: her Eye opes,
> And heaven in it seemes to ope, (that late was shut)
> To take me up to mer[c]y.
>
>   (IV.ii.365–75)

When the Duchess does awake, Bosola, in an action of unmistakable charity, is moved to tell her that her husband is alive.

From this point forward Bosola is penitent, and the whole of Act V is devoted to dramatizing his metamorphosis. Act V has been criticized as an anticlimax, and there can be no question that to some extent it is. After the great concentration of the Duchess's death scene, the diffuse activity of Act V seems wrong. But the failure is one of intensity, not design: Act V is an organic extension of the prison scene, which deepens the focal meaning of the Duchess's experience. The nominal focus in Act V is on Bosola, but Bosola's feelings and actions now serve to dramatize the transforming power of the Duchess and the significance of her suffering and endurance. For though Bosola's mode of action—the old one, the only one he knows, and perhaps the only one possible in a state whose Duke has become a mad dog—though this mode of action cannot express his new feelings, and he ends up killing the one man whose life he is most anxious to preserve, his mistakes are less an indictment of the quality of his regeneration than of the desperate human condition in which it has to be sustained. Right after killing Antonio, Bosola himself seems to realize this:

> (O direfull misprision:)
> I will not Imitate things glorious,
> No more then base: I'll be mine owne example.
> (V.iv.93–95)

Under the circumstances, this is as meaningful a vindication of human integrity as the Duchess's own. Self-destructive madness and animality, literally and powerfully represented by Ferdinand's lycanthropy, flourish in Act V, but they do not, as they do in *The White Devil*, succeed in reducing all human assertions into empty theatrical gestures. The value of the Duchess's humanity, and of Bosola's response to it, is not destroyed.

The difference between *The Duchess* and *The White Devil* in this respect is probably most due to Bosola's role. For Bosola, like Flamineo, is a satirical commentator who has a commanding effect upon the kinds of reactions we have to all the characters and actions he directs or overlooks. When, therefore, he loses part of his sardonic detachment and becomes more deeply implicated in the action, the insistent satiric perspective of the play is ameliorated and even converted to something resembling compassionate insight.

This last point—Webster's conversion of satire, not its simple neutralization—seems to me to be the most distinctive achievement of *The Duchess*. Webster for once has it both ways. He maintains the benefit of satiric dispassion without sacrificing emotional commitment; horror does not obliterate pathos, but at the same time our sense of compassion is required to function in a context which demands a clear consciousness of the limits of compassion. We are, in other words, both engaged and detached, and our resultant distance from the action seems purposeful. The horrible play we watch gradually turns into something we both continue consciously to regard as a fiction and to feel as a dramatic experience. In the last two acts, in fact, this combination is explicitly en-

couraged by images of the theater which are reiterated in both the
language and the action. Early in Act IV the Duchess asks Bosola:

> who must dispatch me?
> I account this world a tedious Theatre
> For I doe play a part in't 'gainst my will.
>   (IV.i.98–100)

Shortly afterwards, she is "plagu'd in Art" by Ferdinand's theatrical
show at the same time that she herself consciously begins to assume a
theatrical role. "Who do I looke like now?" she asks Cariola, and Cariola
answers:

> Like to your picture in the gallery,
> A deale of life in shew, but none in practise:
> Or rather like some reverend monument
> Whose ruines are even pittied;

and the Duchess adds:

> Very proper:
> And Fortune seemes onely to have her eie-sight,
> To behold my Tragedy.
>   (IV.ii.32–38)

The very shape of the prison scene is in some sense like a performance,
with Bosola coaching the Duchess in mortification and helping her
both create and sustain her final part; and so very well does she become
that part that Bosola himself, director if not author, is moved to come
into the play to bring her some comfort and to bear witness to the au-
thenticity of her experience.

Act V is deliberately imagined as a play gone haywire, rife with mistaken cues, confused directions, and actors who can no longer control
their parts. The playwright himself seems to have abdicated. Ferdinand,
who used to be the play's principal author, has taken a madman's role,
and "come[s] to himself," to use Bosola's words, only at the point of
death; the Cardinal is killed in a scene which he helps arrange, when his
followers, prompted by him in advance, ignore what they take to be
his "counterfeiting" cries for help; and Bosola, as he himself realizes,
plays out a villain's part against his will. Ferdinand tells him after the
Duchess's death:

> For thee, (as we observe in Tragedies
> That a good Actor many times is curss'd
> For Playing a villaines part) I hate thee for't.
>   (IV.ii.307–9)

Later, as he is dying, Bosola describes himself as a miscast actor:

> and lastly, for my selfe,
> (That was an Actor in the maine of all,
> Much 'gainst mine owne good nature, yet i' th' end
> Neglected);
>
> (V.v.106–8)

and he accounts for his stabbing of Antonio as the kind of accident which is only natural in the world of a play:

> In a mist: I know not how,
> Such a mistake, as I have often seene
> In a play.
>
> (V.v.118–20)

In such a context, Bosola's resolution "to be [his] owne example" has particular definition and power, and like the Duchess's own self-assertion is at once admirable and profoundly pathetic.

Moody Prior points out that these images of the theater serve to italicize the limitations of human volition and at the same time to give an air of plausibility to the accumulation of intrigue and accidents at the end of the play.[11] But aside from their particular functions, they are also a reflection of Webster's whole self-conscious conception of drama, a conception which was essentially characteristic of the self-regarding comic and tragicomic theater, but which in *The Duchess* he manages, against odds, to convert to the purposes of tragedy. In the last analysis Webster, like most coterie dramatists, wrote plays about plays. In *The White Devil* there is a disjunction between the play he depicts and the play he writes which atrophies any deep involvement either of our emotions or intelligence; in *The Duchess of Malfi* the two plays merge and his dramatic self-consciousness moves more freely in the direction of engagement as well as detachment. In the last acts of *The Duchess*, the artificial and the natural become interchangeable, and, as with the older Elizabethan sense of *theatrum mundi*, the image of the play is dilated into an image of life.

[11] *The Language of Tragedy*, pp. 130–31. For a discussion of theatrical imagery in the *Duchess*, see also Clifford Leech, *Webster: The Duchess of Malfi* (London, 1963), pp. 35–40.

VII

Ford

Ford is the discovery if not the captive of the nineteenth century. Rather conspicuously unnoticed in his own time, he did not merit particular attention from editors and critics until the Romantic period. "Ford was of the first order of poets," wrote Lamb in *Specimens of English Dramatic Poets* (1808). "He sought for sublimity not by parcels in metaphors or visible images, but directly where she has her full residence in the heart of man; in the actions and sufferings of the greatest minds."[1] Specifically, Lamb praised the scene of Calantha's stoic fortitude in *The Broken Heart*, a scene which he said reminded him of Calvary and the Cross. Following Lamb, Ford's first nineteenth-century editor said of *The Broken Heart* that "Few plays possess such an extreme power over the passions, and none in our language can be pointed out superior in pathetic effect"; a few years later, Gifford, in a note to *The Lady's Trial*, remarked upon "that tender feeling which melts the heart in almost every drama of this pathetic writer"; and later in the century, Havelock Ellis, in his introduction to the Mermaid edition (1888), pointed to Ford's celebration of "the burden of a passionate and heavy-laden heart ... the conflict between the world's opinion and the heart's desire." Havelock Ellis also claimed that Ford had necessarily been unpopular since he was the most modern of his contemporaries, less a playwright than an "analyst" who "strained the limits of his art to the utmost" and "foreboded new ways of expression," in particular the novel.[2]

To a remarkable degree, most modern interpretations sympathetic to Ford duplicate these characteristic nineteenth-century views, for where the judgments themselves do not coincide, the ways in which they are formulated do. A standard modern work on Ford views him as the product of a conflict or tension between scientific determinism and unbridled individualism,[3] which is analogous in method, if not in sub-

---

[1] P. 265.

[2] Henry Weber, ed., *The Dramatic Works of John Ford* (London, 1811), p. xxxiii; W. Gifford, ed., *The Dramatic Works of John Ford*, II (London, 1827), 356; Havelock Ellis, ed., *Ford* (London, 1888), pp. xiv, xvi.

[3] George F. Sensabaugh, *The Tragic Muse of John Ford* (Stanford, Cal., 1944). How close Sensabaugh is to 19th-century criticism of Ford may be seen in his claim

stance, to Havelock Ellis's approach, and two of Ford's strongest admirers echo Havelock Ellis in claiming that Ford pushed forward the frontiers of drama to create peculiarly static, if not anti-dramatic plays, designed to explore and analyze "the deep experience of certain emotions."[4] All of Ford's sympathizers admire his worship of the "aristocratic" virtues of "continence, courage and chivalry," and most would agree that in *'Tis Pity She's a Whore*, if not elsewhere, he "dares to find beauty, tenderness, and devotion in a forbidden love."[5]

Interestingly, the comparatively few critics who have reacted against Ford are in more or less conscious rebellion against Romantic assumptions, and not surprisingly they find Ford sentimental and morally unintelligent precisely where his partisans find him admirable. T. S. Eliot thought that all of Ford's plays, except *Perkin Warbeck*, were "meaningless": "a dramatic poet cannot create characters of the greatest intensity of life unless his personages, in their reciprocal actions and behaviour in their story, are somehow dramatizing, but in no obvious form, an action or struggle for harmony in the soul of the poet. In this sense Ford's most famous, though not necessarily best, play may be called 'meaningless.'" Eliot argued also that Ford's poetry, like Beaumont and Fletcher's, is "poetry of the surface: that is to say, it is the result of the stock of expressions of feeling accumulated by greater men."[6]

It seems to me that Eliot's view is the true one but that to be persuasive it must be rescued from the circle of Romantic and anti-Romantic bias that has subsumed the criticism of Ford for the past century and a half. Ford's plays have too often been the vehicles rather than the objects of critical thought and he has been praised and condemned for purposes he probably never intended. Some understanding of his dramaturgical— as opposed to his moral—assumptions is clearly desirable, as is some interpretation of the form rather than the vision of his plays.

The essential point, as Eliot suggested, is Ford's resemblance to Beaumont and Fletcher. Though it is arguable that the final results differ, there can be no question that the characteristic dramatic situations and effects in the plays of Beaumont and Fletcher and of Ford are similar,

---

that "The whole meaning of Ford's plays, in fact, rests on the supremacy of love over all, on the belief that beauty and love should command more respect than convention and law" (p. 165).

[4] Una Ellis-Fermor, *The Jacobean Drama*, p. 235. See also H. J. Oliver, *The Problem of John Ford* (Melbourne, 1955), p. 120.

[5] Ellis-Fermor, op. cit., pp. 235, 236; and Robert Ornstein, *The Moral Vision of Jacobean Tragedy* (Madison, Wis., 1960), p. 210. Similar views of Ford's celebration of aristocratic virtues are found in Clifford Leech, *John Ford and the Drama of his Time* (London, 1957).

[6] *Elizabethan Dramatists* (London, 1953), pp. 125, 132.

if not often identical. Many of the resemblances are very specific. Par-
thenophil-Eroclea, the breeches-part in *The Lover's Melancholy*, frequently acts like Bellario-Euphrasia in *Philaster*, and is placed in comparable predicaments. Bassanes in *The Broken Heart*, an obvious case
of Burtonian jealousy, is akin to Memnon in *The Mad Lover*: both are
equally mad and equally ready to enact a traditional romantic conceit,
Bassanes by boarding up all the windows of his home lest his wife be
subject to lust of the eye, and Memnon by preparing, literally, to offer his
heart to his lady (a kind of literalism demonstrated also in the denoue-
ment of *'Tis Pity*). Bianca's alternating purity and coyness in *Love's
Sacrifice* resembles the behavior of a host of Fletcherian heroines, including Evadne in *The Maid's Tragedy*, and the first boudoir scene between her and Fernando bears some resemblance to the love scene
between Calista and Lisander in Calista's bedroom in *The Lover's
Progress*. Indeed, not only Bianca, but many of Ford's heroines are like
Fletcher's in having "somewhat of Dol Common"[7] in them. In a different key, Calantha's "masculine" courage, so much admired by Lamb,
is probably a deliberate imitation of the "masculine" fortitude of a number of similar ladies in Fletcher's plays, including Ordella in *Thierry
and Theodoret*, and Cleopatra in *The False One*. The debates or rivalry
between friends, Caraffa and Fernando in *Love's Sacrifice*, Auria and
Aurelio in *The Lady's Trial*, are ultimately derivations of the theatrical fashion established by Amintor and Melantius in *The Maid's Tragedy*, and finally, the conflict between love and legal vows which afflicts
Penthea, Bianca, and even Annabella, can be paralleled by such Fletcherian dilemmas as Juliana's rejection of Virolet in *The Double Marriage*, or Calista's of Lisander in *The Lover's Progress*.

The list could easily be continued, but specific parallels do not alone
give an adequate indication of the extent of Ford's debt to Fletcher.
There are probably an equal number of specific Shakespearian echoes in
Ford's play, ranging from the adaptation of the whole of *Romeo and
Juliet* in *'Tis Pity* to scenes and characterizations and speeches in other
plays, and there are in addition many deliberate recollections of lines
and characters from Middleton and Webster, among others.[8] But with
the possible exception of the Shakespearian resonances in *'Tis Pity*, all
of these borrowings tend to be dramatic clichés which Ford exploits
to produce essentially isolated moods or situations or characters. D'Ava-
los in *Love's Sacrifice*, for example, is an obvious copy of Iago, and his

[7] Richard Flecknoe, "A Short Discourse of the English Stage (1664)," *Critical
Essays of the Seventeenth Century*, ed. Spingarn, II, 94.

[8] For a discussion of Ford's Shakespearian borrowings, see Frost, *School of
Shakespeare*, pp. 156–66.

temptation of the Duke is clearly intended to parody Iago's temptation of Othello, but the context in which these imitations are placed inevitably make them stand out as alien and parasitic.

Ford's Fletcherian borrowings, on the other hand, are a reflection and part of a fundamentally Fletcherian orientation. The titles alone of *Love's Sacrifice* and *The Lady's Trial* suggest Fletcherian constructions, and the plays themselves bear out the suggestions. Characteristically, they are, like Fletcher's plays, concerned with acute, ostensibly moral dilemmas, designed to produce alternating or varying states of emotion in the characters and to allow them opportunity for debate and displays of passion. The fulcrum of *Love's Sacrifice* is the triangle of Fernando, Bianca, and the Duke: Fernando, the friend of the Duke, but in love with his wife; Bianca, determined to be faithful to her marriage, but in love with her husband's best friend; the Duke, devoted to both, but torn between jealousy and friendship. As in Fletcher, no dialectical or emotional turn is neglected. Fernando begins by attempting to seduce Bianca and ends as her protector. Bianca first rebuffs him and then says she will give herself to him and commit suicide afterwards. Not surprisingly, Fernando declines, and she then feels free to flirt with him outrageously and to enjoy any liberty short of intercourse. The Duke learns of the affair, and interpreting it incorrectly, he kills Bianca, but then repents when he is convinced by Fernando of her "chastity." There are several more turns at Bianca's tomb: after protracted argument, Fernando commits suicide as a witness to his love for Bianca, and the Duke commits suicide as a witness to his love for both of them.

The Lady's Trial, a tragicomedy, is somewhat less melodramatic, but filled with the same kind of turns and preoccupations. Spinella, the thoroughly true wife of Auria, is tempted by Adurni, but spurns him and convinces him of her great nobility. They are surprised in a private chamber, however, by Auria's friend Aurelio, who misconstrues the scene and reports back to Auria that his honor has been compromised. Instead of a triangle, a quadrilateral results, but there are the same opportunities for debates upon honor (upon rather more fine points, in this instance, as is to be expected of a late Caroline play) and for displays of different and often paradoxically contrasting states of feeling.

Even in *Perkin Warbeck* Ford exploits a romantic triangle as far as the generic requirements of a history play allow. Daliell does not exist in Ford's sources, and much of the interest of the play, even in the strictly historical portions, centers upon the definition of Warbeck's and Lady Katherine's heroism purely in terms of their essentially private love. Warbeck himself, moreover, is a subtle refinement upon the typically Protean Fletcherian character. We know that he is an imposter, but his own passionate belief in his legitimacy almost convinces us that he is not. We are thus made to respond to him and to observe him, to be moved by his speeches and to appreciate them as declamations.

The pattern of *The Broken Heart* is similar, though less transparent and more complicated. The dramatic interest of *The Broken Heart* is distractingly divided between Penthea and Calantha in a way that even the flexibility of Fletcherian plotting cannot resolve, but within their respective plots both Penthea and Calantha are characteristically Fletcherian. Calantha is beset by the conflicting demands of her love for Ithocles and her duty to the state, hardly an uncommon Fletcherian dilemma, and she solves it by remaining true to both, which is the common Fletcherian solution. Her celebrated stoicism is one of the few dialectical and emotional alternatives open to a character in such a position. Another, which Penthea demonstrates, is madness. "A ravished wife, / Widowed," as she explains in witty Fletcherian fashion, "by lawlesse marriage"(IV.ii.146–47), Penthea is successively torn between her duty to a preposterously jealous husband and her love for the man whom her brother forbade her to marry; her psychology, such as it is, is defined almost entirely by the alternation and juxtapositions of these irreconcilable demands.

There are, of course, noticeable differences between Ford's plays and Fletcher's, especially in *'Tis Pity*, which because of its problematic nature will be discussed later in detail. Ford's plays are clearly more decorous, in the Caroline sense. His characters are more consistent; their situations are generally less violently contorted, less prurient (with the exception of *The Fancies Chaste and Noble*), and more plausibly motivated than Fletcher's; the arguments are more finely discriminated; and the juxtapositions are more stylized and geometric. But these are differences of emphasis, not kind, and ones which Ford shares with all of Caroline drama, which is itself less a departure from the practice of Beaumont and Fletcher than an elaboration upon it. Alone they offer no grounds for dissociating Ford from the "heroick way" of drama which Richard Flecknoe saw extending in a continuous tradition from Beaumont and Fletcher to the Restoration.[9]

What would appear to set Ford apart, both from his Caroline contemporaries and from Beaumont and Fletcher, is his pervasive and peculiar use of humours—and this demands rather more detailed consideration. The ultimate source of Ford's humours is Jonson, but whereas in Jonson humours always have primarily moral signification and intellectual effect, in Ford they represent states of feeling and seem more designed to appeal to the audience's motions. The remarkable list of dra-

[9] Op. cit., p. 92.

matis personae in the 1633 edition of *The Broken Heart* makes this shift
very clear. Headed "The Speakers names, fitted to their Qualities," it
describes the characters as follows:

AMYCLAS	*Common to the Kings of Laconia.*
ITHOCLES, *Honour of lovelinesse,*	A favourite.
ORGILUS, *Angry,*	Sonne to Crotolon.
BASSANES, *Vexation,*	A jealous Nobleman.
ARMOSTES, *An Appeaser,*	A Counsellor of State.
CROTOLON, *Noyse,*	Another Counsellor.
PROPHILUS, *Deare,*	Friend to Ithocles.
NEARCHUS, *Young Prince,*	Prince of Argos.
TECNICUS, *Artist,*	A Philosopher.
LEMOPHIL, *Glutton,*	
GRONEAS, *Tavernhaunter,*	} Two Courtiers.
AMELUS, *Trusty,*	Friend to Nearchus.
PHULAS, *Watchfull,*	Servant to Bassanes.
CALANTHA, *Flower of Beauty,*	The Kings daughter.
PENTHEA, *Complaint,*	Sister to Ithocles.
EUPHRANEA, *Joy,*	A Maid of Honor.
CHRISTALLA, *Christall,*	
PHILEMA, *A kisse,*	} Maids of Honour.
GRAUSIS, *Old Beldam,*	Overseer of Penthea.
	Person's included.
THRASUS, *Fiercenesse,*	Father of Ithocles.
APLOTES, *Simplicity,*	Orgilus so disguis'd.

Some of these descriptions, such as "Old Beldam," "Tavernhaunter,"
and "Young Prince," are no more than labels of stock theatrical types,
and others, like "Christall" and "A kisse," are merely fanciful conceits
which are not borne out in the action. But a good number of these qualities really do describe the nature of Ford's characterizations precisely,
for in what amounts to a baroque transformation of the morality play,
personifications of moral states of mind (the traditional conception of
humours) give way to personifications of states of emotion: not jealousy,
but vexation; not pride, but anger; not spiritual resignation, but flower
of beauty; not virtue, but honor of loveliness, or complaint, or joy. The
theatrical behavior of the older morality characters becomes an end
in itself, and as a result the major characterizations of *The Broken Heart*
are defined by sentimental rather than moral qualities. The moral values
of guilt or innocence and virtue or vice are manipulated almost entirely
to create or sustain the dominant emotional traits of the central characters, and the plot is contrived to compose these traits into various designs and counterpoints.

The treatment of Penthea is typical. Her pathos is consistently played

against Bassanes' vexation, Orgilus's anger, and Ithocles' honorable re-
pentence until eventually all four voices form a kind of passionate fugue,
the dominant motif of which is always Penthea's complaint. The fugue
begins with an angry expository recitation by Orgilus (I.i) and proceeds
to a solo of virtually comic vexation by Bassanes (II.i). When Penthea
is introduced (II.i), a duet of vexation and complaint develops between
her and Bassanes, followed later by a duet of complaint and anger when
she rejects Orgilus with a proud but heavy heart:

> 'A sigh'd my name sure as he parted from me,
> I feare I was too rough: Alas poore Gentleman,
> 'A look'd not like the ruines of his youth,
> But like the ruines of those ruines: Honour,
> How much we fight with weaknesse to preserve thee![10]
> (II.iii.127–31)

Immediately after this soliloquy Bassanes enters, and another brief duet
of complaint and vexation further accentuates Penthea's pathos. In the
following act a new duet, one between complaint and honor, is introduced as Ithocles asks his sister's forgiveness for making her marry
Bassanes, and Penthea begins to touch upon the deepest and simultaneously wittiest notes of her complaint:

Pen.   Pray kill me,
>   Rid me from living with a jealous husband;
>   Then we will joyne in friendship, be againe
>   Brother and sister.—Kill me, pray, nay, will 'ee?
Ith. How does thy Lord esteem thee?
Pen.   Such an one
>   As onely you have made me; a faith-breaker,
>   A spotted whore, forgive me, I am one
>   In a[c]t, not in desires, the gods must witnesse.
Ith. Thou dost belye thy friend.
Pen.   I doe not, *Ithocles*;
>   For she that's wife to *Orgilus*, and lives
>   In knowne Adultery with *Bassanes*,
>   Is at best a whore. Wilt kill me now?

>   .   .   .   .   .   .

Ith. After my victories abroad, at home
>   I meet despaire; ingratitude of nature
>   Hath made my actions monstrous: thou shalt stand

---

[10] References to the texts of Ford's plays are to the first editions: *The Broken
Heart* (London, 1633); and *'Tis Pity She's a Whore* (London, 1633). Act, scene,
and line references are to the Regents Drama editions: *The Broken Heart*, ed.
Donald K. Anderson (Lincoln, Neb., 1968); and *'Tis Pity She's a Whore*, ed.
N. W. Bawcutt (Lincoln, Neb., 1966).

A Deity (my sister) and be worship'd
For thy resolved martyrdome: wrong'd maids
And married wives shall to thy hallowed shrine
Offer their orisons, and sacrifice
Pure Turtles, crown'd with mirtle; if thy pitty
Unto a yeelding brothers pressure, lend
One finger but to ease it.
(III.ii.64–75, 80–89)

Ithocles then reveals his own hopeless love for Calantha, and Penthea, despite her own despair, forgives him and offers to help him. At this point, in rushes Bassanes, *"with a ponyard,"* in a state of jealous distraction, and the duet turns into a trio. Afterwards, there is another duet, between complaint and beauty, when Penthea pleads her brother's cause to Calantha (III.v), and to conclude the composition, a final quartet of Penthea, her brother, her husband, and her lover, in which Penthea enters, *"her haire about her eares,"* goading herself with conceits in a final plaint of madness:

There is no peace left for a ravish'd wife
Widdow'd by lawlesse marriage; to all memory,
Penthea's, poor *Penthea's* name is strumpeted:
But since her blood was season'd by the forfeit
Of noble shame, with mixtures of pollution,
Her blood ('tis just) be henceforth never heightned
With tast of sustenance. Starve; let that fulnesse
Whose plurisie hath fever'd faith and modesty,
Forgive me: ô I faint.
(IV.ii.146–54)

This kind of musical design, which is typical of Ford's drama, is not without its own peculiar power and subtlety, but it should be understood for what it is. If it has a "rhythm of lyric feeling," that rhythm is "tragic" only in a very special sense, and there seems little warrant for interpreting the feelings themselves as "memorable affirmations of the spirit."[11] For Ford's emotional rhythm is finally only a variation of the Fletcherian pattern, and *The Broken Heart* is in substance and design an essentially Fletcherian drama. Such beliefs as it represents are no more than decorative conceits of Caroline chivalry, and even they are invoked not to be explored but to provide the skeleton for the portrayal of a variety of emotions composed in a variety of spatial patterns. Penthea is in every sense the descendant of Aspatia: she has the same kind of emotional appeal and the same kind of dramatic function; and *The Broken Heart* is designed to italicize that appeal in just the way that

[11] Ornstein, op. cit., pp. 201, 199.

The Maid's Tragedy is designed to set off the passion of Aspatia. Penthea is represented with greater concentration than Aspatia, and *The Broken Heart* in general is more emotional and less witty than *The Maid's Tragedy*, but the essential Fletcherian pattern remains unchanged. Even in the extremity of grief Penthea is characterized by verbal wit, since her grief is itself the creation of her consciousness of the paradoxes of her dilemma; and in exploiting emotion as it does, the play as a whole merely intensifies an inherent potential of the Fletcherian form. The only significant departure from Fletcher in *The Broken Heart* is the failure to achieve a satisfactory arrangement for an unusually diffuse cast of qualities.

Interestingly, Lamb may have been the first to recognize the affinity of Ford and Fletcher, although he was not conscious of doing so. Writing of the scene in which Fletcher's Ordella heroically prepares to be killed by her unwitting husband, he remarked in a passage from which we have already quoted:

> I have always considered this to be the finest scene in Fletcher, and Ordella the most perfect idea of the female heroic character, next to Calantha in the *Broken Heart* of Ford, that has been embodied in fiction. She is a piece of sainted nature. Yet noble as the whole scene is, it must be confessed that the manner of it, compared with Shakespeare's finest scenes, is slow and languid. Its motion is circular, not progressive. Each line resolves on itself in a sort of separate orbit. They do not join into one another like a running hand. Every step that we go we are stopped to admire some single object, like walking in beautiful scenery with a guide. This slowness I shall have occasion elsewhere to remark as characteristic of Fletcher. Another striking difference perceivable between Fletcher and Shakespeare, is the fondness of the former for unnatural and violent situations, like that in the scene before us. He seems to have thought that nothing could be produced in the ordinary way. The chief incidents in the *Wife for a Month*, in *Cupid's Revenge*, in the *Double Marriage*, and in many more of his Tragedies, shew this. Shakespeare had nothing of this contortion of mind, none of that craving after romantic incidents, and flights of strained and improbable virtue, which I think always betrays an imperfect moral sensibility.[12]

Lamb clearly did not intend this as a description of Ford—though his association of Calantha and Ordella is suggestive—but it surely applies as justly to Ford as to Fletcher. Both have the same kinds of dialectical and emotional dilemmas (and contortions), the same kinds of characterizations, and the same slow circularity of motion. The statuesque quality which many critics admire in Ford's plays, and which even Eliot admired in his verse, is no more than an adumbration of the self-

[12] *Specimens of English Dramatic Poets*, pp. 403–4.

conscious revolving motion which Lamb so perceptively saw to be the basis of Fletcherian tragicomic dramaturgy. Such dramaturgy need not, of course, be stigmatized as the product of an imperfect moral sensibility, but neither can it seriously be interpreted as a breakthrough to the frontiers of drama. Ford's plays are theatrical to their core, and there seems no reason to make more pretentious claims for them than most critics are prepared to make for the plays of Fletcher.

The one possible exception to this judgment is *'Tis Pity She's a Whore*, a play which we must now consider. *'Tis Pity* is in important respects different from Ford's other plays, and the clearest sign and explanation of the difference is the extent and quality of its debt to Shakespeare, for rather than echoing discrete lines or characters or moods from Shakespeare, as was his usual practice, in *'Tis Pity* Ford sought to adapt the conception of an entire play. He does not merely recollect *Romeo and Juliet*, but attempts to rework it, to translate it, into terms which will be viable both for his own dramatic temperament and for the expectations of his Caroline audience.

This goal, and his partial success in achieving it, produces some interesting consequences. For the first and only time in his dramatic career, Ford tells something resembling a continuous story: what happens next and how it happens are at least as important as spatial relationships of events and emotions, and the laws of cause and effect operate upon both the characters and the action. The result is that alone among Ford's characters Giovanni and Annabella to some extent develop rather than just change. Giovanni's passion may be presented as a *fait accompli*, an emotional state without particularized motivation, but the spiritual degeneration of his love is represented gradually, as the natural and inevitable consequence of incest. His violation of custom, his possession of Annabella, leads progressively and logically to his alienation from any accepted order, his usurpation of the role of fate, and his final desire literally to possess Annabella's soul. Annabella's repentance, though less well realized, is comparably related to the consequences of her incestuous relationship: she becomes pregnant and must marry a man whom she does not love, and with the friar's help, comes to understand that regardless of her feelings, or rather because of them, her soul stands in peril of damnation.

The relationship of Giovanni and Annabella to one another and to society is also unusual in that it constitutes a thematic organization for the play as a whole rather than just a pattern or decorative conceit. Almost all the episodes and characters in *'Tis Pity*, even those of low comedy (never distinguished in Ford by their relevance), bear directly upon the love of Giovanni and Annabella, and upon its significance. Soranzo's perfidy to Hippolita and her responding Machiavellianism, for example, not only help establish sympathy for the integrity of the incestuous lovers but also dramatize the corruption of customary form which makes incest emotionally if not morally explicable. The Cardinal's mundane travesty of justice and Bergetto's idiotic parody of love exercise a similar function. The extent to which the variant parts of *'Tis Pity* are thus metaphorically unified is most unusual for Ford.

A final, and perhaps the most important, Shakespearian influence is evident in the poetry of *'Tis Pity*. Ford's verse often has distinction, but there is a special quality about the dramatic poetry of *'Tis Pity* which suggests the salutary example of Shakespeare's integration of language and action. In Ford's other plays the celebrated passages are essentially arias, capable indeed of range and power, but almost always static, unrelated to the preceding or succeeding action, unrelated sometimes even to the immediate context. In *'Tis Pity*, on the other hand, much of the best verse depends intimately upon the context of action and is richer and more powerful because it does. A good example is Annabella's speech to her brother at the end of the play imploring him to prepare for death:

> Brother, deare brother, know what I have beene,
> And know that now there's but a dining time
> Twixt us and our Confusion: let's not waste
> These precious houres in vayne and uselesse speech.
> Alas, these gay attyres were not put on
> But to some end; this suddaine solemne Feast
> Was not ordayn'd to riott in expence;
> I that have now beene chambred here alone,
> Bard of my Guardian, or of any else,
> Am not for nothing at an instant free'd
> To fresh accesse; be not deceiv'd *My Brother,*
> This Banquet is an harbinger of Death
> To you and mee, resolve your selfe it is,
> And be prepar'd to welcome it.
>   (V.v.16–29)

The limpidity of this speech is characteristic of all of Ford's verse at its best, but the urgency and power which this quiet clarity assumes in this instance is special and is a function of the exceptional extent to which Ford roots the speech in the action of the immediate scene as well as of the play as a whole. The speech expresses not only Annabella's feelings, but the situation and context which gives rise to them. Behind the phrase, "Brother, deare brother," lie the history of their whole incestuous relationship and the poignancy of her present attempt to salvage from its corruption at least the affection of a sister; and behind all the references to the banquet lies her awareness, as lucid as the rhythm of her speech, of what she and Giovanni have become and of the fate which awaits them. There is no dramatic verse in Ford's other plays which is at once so unpretentious and so penetrating.

'Tis Pity thus, in both its verse and structure, enjoys a distinction in Ford's canon which it seems to owe to the stimulus of the Shakespearian example. But at the same time there is at least an equally important Fletcherian impulse in the play which must also be fully appreciated. The incestuous relationship itself poses precisely the kind of dilemma which Fletcher usually exploited and which Ford himself often treated in his other plays: love versus, in Giovanni's words, "customary form." In Ford's other plays the customary form is usually marriage and the love involves a third party, usually a friend of the husband; in *'Tis Pity* the triangle is compressed into a relationship between two people which contains potentially all the dramatic forces which operate among three. Giovanni is at once the brother of Annabella, the guardian of her honor, and her lover, and Annabella both loves Giovanni as a brother for whose salvation she is concerned and as a lover whom she desires. Ford dramatizes most of the possible combinations of these roles, each combination characteristically providing occasion for debate or passionate declamation; and when both Giovanni and Annabella appear to have resolved their respective dualities Ford introduces a real husband, Soranzo, who reestablishes and exacerbates most of the conflicts.

With sufficient virtuosity, of course, any dramatic situation can be construed as "Fletcherian": on the surface, for example, Romeo and Juliet are faced with as Fletcherian a dilemma as Giovanni and Annabella. Theirs too is a love proscribed by their society, and Shakespeare is certainly interested in the resultant conflict. The difference, however, is that in *Romeo and Juliet* the dilemma is subsumed in the story and is finally subsidiary to the characterizations and feelings which the story as a whole creates, whereas in *'Tis Pity* the dilemma is often valued in the Fletcherian manner, as a precipitant for essentially discrete juxtapositions of emotion and argument. Perhaps the clearest instance is the quarrel scene between Annabella and Soranzo (IV.iii). Soranzo enters, "*unbrac't*," dragging Annabella after him. In a rage he accuses her of being a "famous whoore, . . . rare, notable Harlot," and demands the reason why he was chosen to be her cuckold. Annabella answers:

> Beastly man, why 'tis thy fate:
> I sued not to thee, for, but that I thought
> Your *Over-loving Lordship* would have runne
> Madd on denyall, had yee lent me time,
> I would have told 'ee in what case I was.
> But you would needs be doing.

Soran.   Whore of whores!
          Dar'st thou tell mee this?
Anna.   O yes, why not?
          You were deceiv'd in mee; 'twas not for love
          I chose you, but for honour; yet know this,
          Would you be patient yet, and hide your shame,
          I'de see whether I could love you.
                                        (IV.iii.1, 15–24)

Further enraged, Soranzo demands that Annabella tell him who has
made her pregnant. She refuses and continues to taunt him:

          Soft, sir, 'twas not in my bargaine.
          Yet somewhat sir to stay your longing stomacke
          I'm content t'acquaint you with; *The man,*
          The more than *Man* that got this sprightly Boy,
          (For 'tis a Boy that for glory sir,
          Your heyre shalbe a Sonne.)
Soran.   Damnable Monster!
Anna. Nay and you will not heare, I'le speake no more.
Soran. Yes speake, and speake thy last.
Anna.   A match, a match;
          This *Noble Creature* was in every part
          So angell-like, so glorious, that a woeman,
          Who had not been but human as was I,
          Would have kneel'd to him, and have beg'd for love.
          You, why you are not worthy once to name
          His name without true worship, or indeede,
          Unlesse you kneel'd, to heare another name him.
Soran. What was he cal'd?
Anna.   We are not come to that,
          Let it suffice that you shall have the glory
          To *Father* what so *Brave a Father got.*
                                        (ll. 28–45)

Soranzo continues to demand the name of the man, swearing at one
point, "I'le ripp up thy heart, / And finde it there" (ll. 53–54). He is in
fact about to kill her when Vasques enters with a more Machiavellian
policy, and the scene takes a new turn. Soranzo acts forgiving, Annabella
becomes contrite, and eventually the information is extracted from
Putana.

    This scene is not unrelated to the action of the rest of the play. Anna-
bella's behavior can be construed as an expression of her despair and her
desire to goad Soranzo into killing her,[13] and Soranzo's remark about

---

[13] Introduction to *'Tis Pity*, ed. Bawcutt, p. xxi.

ripping her heart out is an ironic anticipation of Giovanni's later act. But the real emphasis of the scene is nonetheless upon sensational argument in the Fletcherian mode. Whatever her motives, Annabella sounds and behaves in this scene exactly like Bianca in *Love's Sacrifice*, and as with Bianca, her impudent wit and defiance mark her unmistakably as one of the progeny of Beaumont and Fletcher's Evadne. The whole shape of the scene suggests a variation upon the archetypal bedroom scene between Amintor and Evadne, and a necessarily sensational one at that, since instead of being the King's mistress, Annabella is the mistress of her brother, and is in addition pregnant.

In principle there is no reason why Ford could not use such a Fletcherian situation for new and perhaps more penetrating purposes, or why he could not integrate it into a play constructed largely on other grounds. But in fact he does neither. Annabella's argument is exploited for the same shock value as Evadne's or Bianca's and makes little contribution to our understanding of the action or of her character. On the contrary, her impudence, though not implausible under the circumstances, conveys an impression which conflicts with what we have seen of her earlier in the play and which seriously interferes with our acceptance of what happens to her at the end of the play. In contrast to Giovanni, Annabella is neither proud nor insensitive to the demands of religion, and her characterization seems intended to suggest a woman gradually becoming aware of the nature and enormity of her sin. Shortly before her argument with Soranzo she is shown with the friar, looking for a way "to redeeme [her] miseries," (III.vii.33) and shortly after the argument she is shown with the friar again, fully repentant. At best, her impudence and wit are out of place in this development, and at worst, they actually subvert its continuity. In the case of Evadne or Bianca we accept such shifts of emotion and attitude because they are part of a fully articulated pattern of Protean dramaturgy, but Annabella's peripetetic behavior cannot be accommodated to any single governing pattern, which is why it is disturbing.

It is also why the play itself is disturbing, for as with Annabella, *'Tis Pity* as a whole is influenced by two different kinds of dramaturgy and suffers from the competition between them. There is no moral confusion, as such, in *'Tis Pity*—that issue has always been a red herring. As a number of critics have noticed, the play is studded with orthodox references to the idolatrous nature of the incestuous passion, to the sinful pride of the lovers (especially of Giovanni), and to the ultimate power which "Heaven" exerts in the earthly affairs of the play.[14] The Friar is a vehicle for such sentiments, as is Richardetto later in the play,

[14] See especially Mark Stavig, *John Ford and the Traditional Moral Order* (Madison, Wis., 1968), pp. 95–121.

and both of them make direct comments upon the action. But the difficulty is that the moral understanding which these comments and references are designed to create does not always move in the same direction or in the same way as the play's theatrical effects. It is possible that this disjunction is a necessary consequence of Ford's exaggeration of the *Romeo and Juliet* story, or it may be that he was naturally drawn to the Fletcherian potential of that story, but in any event *'Tis Pity* is often sensational and theatrically self-indulgent.

Annabella's defiance is the most unambiguous example of this self-indulgence, but there are others. The friar's sentiments are so often both obvious and lurid that they operate primarily as a contrast to Giovanni's displays of sophistry and passion. Richardetto's comments are also largely ornamental, since despite his orthodoxy, his own motives are those of revenge. Most important, like Annabella, and more often than she, Giovanni revels as much in his own rhetoric as in his passion—this is the theatrical burden of all his debates with the friar and of many of those with Annabella—and although this preciosity is not necessarily incompatible with the moral outlines of the story, it receives an emphasis which sets it apart from the story if not against it. Indeed, as often as the emotions and arguments of both Annabella and Giovanni are generated by the action, they are also portrayed discretely and discontinuously. As a result, it is frequently impossible to reconcile the theatrical emphasis of *'Tis Pity* with the purported moral or psychological significance of its plot, and the play ultimately suffers from an unresolved conflict of dramatic interests.

Conclusion

"THE plays of Beaumont and Fletcher," wrote Coleridge, "are mere aggregations without unity; in the Shakespearian drama there is a vitality which grows and evolves itself from within—a keynote which guides and controls the harmonies throughout."[1] This is a familiar charge, not unlike Lamb's, and in some respects an invidious one. Fletcherian plays may not grow like Shakespeare's, but they are not therefore without vitality, and though they are often aggregations, they are not therefore without unity. Nevertheless, Coleridge's distinction is true as well as important, for the harmonies of plays written on Shakespearian principles and of those written on Fletcherian principles are different both in kind and dimension, and an appreciation of the differences is essential for a just understanding of the history of seventeenth-century drama.

Most of these differences have already been discussed, but it is worth gathering them together to suggest their implications in some historical perspective. It is best to begin by shifting from Coleridge's Romantic image of an organism to an analogous but more Elizabethan metaphor of dramatic Providence. Essentially, the plays of Shakespeare and his early contemporaries are informed by a Boethian conception of Fate and Providence, the former an understanding of human events having discernible causes and effects in time, the latter an heavenly or super-natural disposition of events which exists outside time in an eternal present. The medieval cycle plays were about the eternal present and represented it directly. The English shepherds in *The Second Shepherds' Play* are continuous in time (and place) with the shepherds outside Bethlehem, as the mock birth of Mak's stolen sheep is with Christ's nativity. The beginning and end of the play, the literal story and its "meaning" are coextensive. In Elizabethan plays Christ himself has disappeared, but a providential or supernatural meaning of what have now become secular stories remains to govern the configuration of the story and of our response to it. *The Spanish Tragedy* represents the transition almost diagrammatically. Hieronimo's fate, his grief and quest for justice, are fully realized in literal terms, but they are surrounded and

---

[1] *Lectures and Notes on Shakspere and other English Poets*, ed. T. Ashe (London, Bohn ed., 1883), p. 400.

punctuated by a supernatural framework which makes us explicitly aware of causes which he cannot see and of a pattern to his action, operating like Providence, of which he cannot be conscious. We consequently experience the play more or less as the Ghost of Andrea does: we have a foot in two worlds. We respond to the human story in human terms, but we also see, as its participants do not, the point towards which it is predestined to move, the principle which governs its evolution.

In later Elizabethan plays the providential framework recedes from view as the human story acquires more autonomy, but as a number of critics have shown, it still inheres in the action, determining both the ways in which plays are constructed and the nature of our response to them. The ubiquitous double plots (direct descendants of the coextensive stories of the mystery plays) and a physical stage with flexible definitions of time and space, capable of being realistic and symbolic at the same time, are among the many means which combine to communicate a sense of "an unseen referent at [the] center" of Elizabethan plays and to create a response which includes an extraordinary capacity for simultaneous sympathy and judgment, engagement and detachment.[2]

Perhaps the clearest contemporary expression of this capacity was the metaphor of *theatrum mundi*.[3] In the Middle Ages the metaphor was a means of describing man's role in a universe created and directed by God, and it was not employed in the drama itself; but as Erich Auerbach remarked,[4] just at the point where Christ's story was no longer the ostensive subject of the drama, classical precedents of dramatic structure replaced the stipulated form of Christian history and the metaphor of the theater of the world began to be applied in the other direction. If the world was like the theater, then the theater was also like the world (physically as well as figuratively, with its own heavens, middle earth, and hell); and the dramatist's power and art was like that of Providence. It is this association, both substantive and formal, of the dramatist and God which allows us to dilate our consciousness of the play in

[2] Bernard Beckerman, *Shakespeare at the Globe* (New York, 1962), p. 62. Among the host of articles and books on this aspect of Elizabethan dramaturgy, see also William Empson, "Double Plots," *Some Versions of Pastoral* (London, 1935); Erich Auerbach, *Mimesis*, trans. Willard Trask (Princeton, N.J., 1953), pp. 274–93; and Maynard Mack, "Engagement and Detachment in Shakespeare's Plays," *Essays on Shakespeare and Elizabethan Drama in Honor of Hardin Craig*, ed. Hosley (Columbia, Mo., 1962), pp. 275–96.

[3] See especially Ernst Curtius, *European Literature and the Latin Middle Ages*, trans. Willard Trask (New York, 1953), pp. 138–44; Richard Bernheimer, "Theatrum Mundi," *The Art Bulletin*, XXXVIII (1956), pp. 225–47; and Anne Righter, *Shakespeare and the Idea of the Play* (London, 1962), pp. 59–78.

[4] *Mimesis*, p. 279.

Elizabethan drama, and it is when it is effectively lost, when the play is no longer sustained by metaphysical reverberations, when Providence disappears as a principle of structure as well as belief, that the drama begins to experience the effects which we have been examining in this study. Satirical comedy, tragicomedy, and the coterie theater itself are at once symptoms and sources of this process.

The ultimate termination of these developments was celebrated, paradoxically, by Rymer, his own thinking unmistakably a product of the Fletcherian tradition he deplored, in his notion of "poetical justice," a dispensation in which the play becomes almost entirely scrutable and drained of metaphor, but the drama had changed, clearly and fundamentally, many years earlier. *'Tis Pity She's a Whore* (1629?–33) is the last significant play of what Dryden called the "Gyant Race, before the Flood." Ford's late Jacobean and Caroline contemporaries—public theater dramatists like Massinger and Shirley, as well as court playwrights like Cartwright—are all essentially epigones of Fletcher, who merely codified his lessons and helped transmit them to the Restoration. Massinger, one of Fletcher's chief collaborators and his successor as principal dramatist for the King's Men, was almost totally parasitic, and at his worst actually managed to exaggerate Fletcher's theatrical narcissism. In his play *The Roman Actor*, for example, the majority of the big scenes are literally performed by the central protagonist, the Roman actor of the title, for various audiences within the play, until ultimately the whole drama is reduced to a mindless solipsism. Shirley, with more talent, had a greater capacity to vary or heighten the conventional formulae, but he did not change or extend them. His own astute criticism of the characteristics of Fletcherian drama in the preface to the Beaumont and Fletcher folio is also a perfect description of the premises and effects of his own plays. His tragicomedy *The Young Admiral*, which was extravagantly admired by Caroline audiences, is typical: composed of a series of ingenious turns and counterturns, providing almost limitless occasions for debate and declamatory displays of passion, it is entirely contrived to make the spectator "admire the subtile trackes of [his] engagement."[5] The same is true of the court plays of the period. Cavalier dramas like Cartwright's *The Royal Slave* have more emphasis upon debate than action and generally more preciosity than those in the contemporary public theater, but their dramatic assumptions are similarly Fletcherian. Like Restoration heroic plays, they simply took the Fletcherian interest in design to an extreme, becoming increasingly like the formal gardens to which the dramatists often compared them.[6]

[5] See above, Chap. IV, for the complete quotation from Shirley's preface.
[6] For a discussion of the relationship of Cavalier drama both to earlier Fletch-

Not long after the closing of the theaters, Sir William Davenant, in his preface to *Gondibert* (1651), summed up the characteristics of the "regular species" of English drama of which he himself was one of the most influential practitioners. His description reads very much like a Fletcherian version of the *pièce bien faite* and is an indication of how greatly the theater of the world had become contracted by the middle of the century:

The first *Act* is the general preparative, by rendring the chiefest characters of persons, and ending with something that looks like an obscure promise of design. The second begins with an introducement of new persons, so finishes all the characters, and ends with some little performance of that design which was promis'd at the parting of the first *Act*. The third makes a visible correspondence in the under-walks (or lesser intrigues) of persons; and ends with an ample turn of the main design, and expectation of a new. The fourth (ever having occasion to be the longest) gives a notorious turn to all the under-walks, and a counterturn to that main design which was chang'd in the third. The fifth begins with an intire diversion of the main, and dependant Plotts; then makes the general correspondence of the persons more discernable, and ends with an easy untying of those particular knots, which made a contexture of the whole; leaving such satisfaction of probabilities with the Spectator, as may perswade him that neither Fortune in the fate of the Persons, nor the Writer in the Representment, have been unnatural or exorbitant.[7]

Davenant of course is describing the mechanics of the form, not its possibilities. That a drama based upon such principles of design is capable of its own integrity, power, and development needs no further argument. If we make no more pretences for them than they make for themselves, the ends of Fletcherian tragicomedy are neither unworthy nor unimportant, and as we have seen, when they are directed towards comedy their results are especially significant. The achievement of Restoration comedy was made possible precisely when the fate of men had become almost entirely intelligible as a function of their social behavior rather than of the state of their souls, and when the dynamics of their relationships, like the power of the "Writer" himself, had become less a function of great creating Nature than of human artifice. The world of Restoration comedy is the first really secular world in English drama, and for its representation the principles of Fletcherian dramaturgy, in-

---

erian plays and to the later heroic drama, see Arthur C. Kirsch, *Dryden's Heroic Drama* (Princeton, N.J., 1965), pp. 70–72 and passim.

[7] (London, 1651), pp. 23–24. For a discussion of this quotation, as well as of Davenant's work in the Caroline and Restoration theater, see *Dryden's Heroic Drama*, pp. 15–22 and passim.

cluding a detritus of the tradition of satirical comedy which lay behind Fletcher, were exactly right.

At the same time, it is equally important to recognize that the impingement of this dramaturgy and its antimetaphysical premises and implications upon the work of Jacobean dramatists who were still in part children of an earlier tradition produced results which were not always salutary and which should be carefully distinguished. For Marston, Webster, and Ford the results are mixed. The plays in which they are able, at least partially, to unite theatrical self-consciousness with some commitment to traditional ideas of dramatic Providence, are their best works; those in which this commitment, though invoked, is not real, suffer from preciosity.

Middleton fared better. Capitalizing successfully on the coterie theater in which he was trained, he from the first and in all his plays devoted his energies to an essentially psychomachic drama in which actors on the stage of man's soul cast relentless shadows upon the actors, men and women of the time, on the stage of the seventeenth-century theater, and the detachment bred of the palimpsest of these two stages leads to a sense of irony in word play and action that is not only far from precious but a function of profound moral insight. The achievement is, to be sure, reactionary and costly. Middleton's irony is satirically reductive as well as harsh, deliberately cauterizing our responses, and partly as a consequence the range of experience he is capable of exploring is narrow. The spaciousness of Elizabethan metaphor is not accessible to him —it is symptomatic that the analogies between the two plots of *The Changeling* are drawn at the end of the play with unusual explicitness— and there is really no heaven in his providential histories. But within these limits he is a master, without equal in the clinical depiction in both language and action of the roles forced upon men by their folly and viciousness.

Shakespeare alone was able to respond to the new theatrical developments in the later part of his career in a way that still fully exploited the old tradition in which he had been bred and to which his own earlier plays were the greatest testimony. The consciousness of theater and theatrical form in both the problem comedies and last plays is acute but at the same time constantly and profoundly enriched by associations of the dramatist's creative process with that of Nature and of the providence of his tragicomic design with the Providence that embraces his characters and audience alike. The result is a drama whose argument of wonder confirms the truth as well as the possibilities of our own experience.

Index

Aristotle, 8, 9
Armstrong, William A., 5n, 20n
Auerbach, Erich, 128

Barker, Richard H., 77n
Baskervill, C. R., 16n
Bawcutt, N. W., 124n
Beaumont and Fletcher, 3, 4, 6, 7, 9, 14,
    38–51, 57, 58, 62, 65, 66, 67, 96, 97–98,
    104, 105, 113–16, 119–21, 123–26, 127,
    129–31
    Maid's Tragedy, 42–47, 49, 101, 119–
        20, 125
    Philaster, 40–42, 43, 47
Beckerman, Bernard, 128n
Bentley, G. E., 4n, 5n, 52n
Bernheimer, Richard, 128n
Bevington, David, 22n
Boethius, 127
Bogard, Travis, 100n
Brackman, Jacob, 29n
Bradbrook, Muriel, 62n, 101n
Brown, John Russell, 97n, 101–2

Campbell, O.J., 4n
Caputi, Anthony, 20n, 27n
Cartwright, 129
Chapman, 4, 97
Coleridge, 47, 127
Congreve, 51
Craik, T. W., 22n
Curtius, Ernst, 128n

Danby, John F., 43, 46–47
Davenant, 130
Davenport, Arnold, 31n
David, Richard, 60n
Davison, Peter, 41n
Dessen, Alan C., 23n
Dryden, 3, 51, 129

Edwards, Philip, 62n
Eliot, T. S., 47, 75, 113, 120
Ellis, Havelock, 112, 113
Ellis-Fermor, Una, 59n, 113n
Empson, William, 128n
Enck, John H., 19n
Engelberg, Edward, 85n

Fergusson, Francis, 105n
Finkelpearl, Philip J., 20n, 21n, 27, 28,
    29, 35n, 86n
Flecknoe, Richard, 114n, 116
Foakes, R. A., 27n
Ford, 3, 45, 51, 112–26, 131
    Broken Heart, 116–21
    'Tis Pity She's a Whore, 113, 121–
        26, 129
Franklin, H. Bruce, 104n
Frost, David L., 4n, 114n
Frye, Northrop, 72n

Gibbons, Brian, 4n
Gifford, W., 112
Granville-Barker, H., 65, 66–67, 73
Guarini, 7–15, 32, 37, 38, 57, 58, 59, 62,
    64, 67

Harbage, Alfred, 4, 5n
Harris, Bernard, 32n, 74n
Henning, Standish, 87n
Heroic drama, 116, 129–30
Herrick, Marvin T., 6n, 7n
Hillebrand, H. N., 5n
Holmes, David M., 77n
Horace, 15
Hunter, G. K., 20n, 27–28, 35n, 54n, 63

Johnson, Samuel, 52
Jonson, 3, 4, 5, 7, 15–24, 28, 38, 39, 54,
    81, 88, 96, 97, 104, 116
    Cynthia's Revels, 18–22
    Every Man out of His Humour, 4,
        5, 15–18

Kay, W. David, 15n
Kermode, Frank, 66n
Kernan, Alvin, 6n, 19n
Kimbrough, Robert, 52n
Kirsch, Arthur C., 4n, 42n, 74n, 129n,
     130n
Knight, G. Wilson, 63
Knights, L. C., 6n
Kyd, 16, 127–28

Lamb, 44, 112, 114, 120, 127
Lawrence, W. W., 54n
Leech, Clifford, 54n, 101n, 111n, 113n
Leishman, J. B., 86n
Levin, Richard, 77n
Lyly, 14

Mack, Maynard, 128n
Marston, 4, 20, 25–37, 39, 58, 62, 65–66,
     67, 98, 104, 131
     Malcontent, 31, 32–37, 66, 98, 102–3
Massinger, 51, 129
Middleton, 4, 5, 20, 24, 51, 75–96, 104,
     114, 131
     Changeling, 80, 82–83, 84–85, 86,
          131
     Hengist, 79, 82, 83
     Mad World, My Masters, 77–78, 81,
          84, 86–90, 92
     Michaelmas Term, 75, 76–77, 78,
          81, 83, 86, 87n, 92–93
     Women Beware Women, 76–77, 79–
          80, 82–83, 84, 86, 90–92, 93–95
Mincoff, Marco, 6n
Moore, Don D., 97n
Morality play:
     and Jonson, 20–23
     and Middleton, 80–96

Norland, Howard, 46n

Oliver, H. J., 113n
Orgel, Stephen, 23n
Ornstein, Robert, 113n, 119n

Parker, R. B., 84n
Peter, John, 31n
Pirandello, 27, 31
Price, Hereward T., 107n
Price, Joseph G., 52n
Prior, Moody, 97, 111

Rabkin, Norman, 74n
Redwine, James, 21n

Restoration comedy, 3, 48, 51, 130–31
Ribner, Irving, 101n
Ricks, Christopher, 80
Righter, Anne, 128n
Ristine, F. H., 6n
Rymer, 3, 45–46, 129

Satirical comedy, 4, 6, 131
     and Beaumont and Fletcher, 38
     and Jonson, 15–24
     and Middleton, 75–96 *passim*
     and Webster, 98
Schoenbaum, Samuel, 84n
Second Shepherds' Play, 127
Sensabaugh, George F., 112n
Shakespeare, 3, 5, 6, 12, 14, 24, 36, 44,
     46, 48, 51, 52–74, 96, 97, 98, 105,
     114–15, 120–23, 126, 127, 131
     All's Well That Ends Well, 52–64,
          67, 68, 72, 73, 74
     Cymbeline, 5, 64–74
Shapiro, Michael, 5n, 20n
Shirley, 39–40, 51, 129
Simeone, Walter F., 7n
Smith, Irwin, 5n
Sophocles, 10
Southern, Richard, 17n
Spivack, Bernard, 22n, 81n
Staton, William E., 7n
Stavig, Mark, 125n

Theatrum mundi, 24, 111, 128–29
Tomlinson, T. B., 83n, 101n
Tragicomedy:
     and Beaumont and Fletcher, 3, 4, 5,
          6, 7, 38–51
     and Ford, 112–26 *passim*
     and Guarini, 7–15
     and Middleton, 78–79, 81–82, 95–96
     and Shakespeare, 3, 6, 52–74
     and Webster, 97–111 *passim*
Turner, Robert Y., 62n

Waith, Eugene M., 6n, 38n, 39, 50n
Wallis, Lawrence B., 4n
Weber, Henry, 112n
Webster, 4, 20, 45, 51, 97–111, 114, 131
     Duchess of Malfi, 106–11
     White Devil, 97–106, 107, 108, 111
Wells, Stanley, 74n
Wilson, Edmund, 19
Wright, Abraham, 4n, 42n